# ForeTalk

*The 7 Critical Conversations
for Living in the Season of Now*

## STAN CRAIG

**FORETALK**
The 7 Critical Conversations for Living in the Season of Now
Copyright © 2013 by STANLEY L .CRAIG

All scripture quotations, except where indicated, are from THE MESSAGE.
Copyright 1993,1994,1995,1996, 2000, 2001, 2002, 2005.
Used by permission of the NavPress Publishing Group.

Published by Legacy Publishing Group, 10604 Jinson St., Prospect, KY 40059

**ISBN-10: 0985335653   ISBN-13: 978-0-9853356-5-6**

Cover and Interior Design: Leana Santana
Photo and Illustration Credit: Leana Santana, Istockphoto.com
Author Photo Credit: Midtown Photo, Sacramento, CA

DISCLAIMER: The materials in this book represent the views and opinions of the author, who is not an attorney, and should not be construed to be the opinions of the firms, organizations, churches, foundations or individuals who may be in association with, employ or relate to the author or distribute this material. This book is neither construed to be legal advice, medical advice or guidance nor advice from an insurance professional, funeral director, either generally or specifically, in regard to any case, financial plan, or funeral plan. The reader is responsible to consult his or her own attorney and other professionals for specific guidance and advice. This book and any forms or agreements herein are for educational and informational purposes only. The names were changed in every illustration or example in the text, except for author's brother Ronald Craig, and do not represent any specific person or family either living or dead.

This book and all audio and video components are sold with the understanding that the views expressed herein are for informational purposes only and that the author is not engaged in or rendering any form or type of legal advice.

ForeTalk, the ForeTalk Seminar and its author assumes no responsibility for errors, inaccuracies or omissions that may appear in this publication. The Author reserves the right to change this publication at any time without notice. ForeTalk and the ForeTalk Seminar cannot in any way guarantee that the forms, templates and information enclosed herein and including and specifically the guide and notebook are being used for the purpose intended and therefore assumes no responsibility for their proper and correct use.

*"**All my life I was taught how to die as a Christian, but no one ever taught me how I ought to live in the years before I die. I wish they had...**"*

- Billy Graham, *Nearing Home*, 2011

# PRAISE FOR FORETALK:

*The 7 Critical Conversations for Living in the Season of Now*

"Younger people should be inspired by the practical, hopeful manner in which mature Christians prepare for the end of life. However, many miss this opportunity to share their belief and convictions because we have not been told how. Stan Craig's book, **_ForeTalk_** gives helpful counsel about **how to make the final phase of life both a blessing for your family and a powerful witness for Christ.**"

> — BOB RUSSELL
> *Founding Pastor, Southeast Christian Church*
> *Author of 11 books including, When God Builds a Church and Blessed Are The Caregivers.*

"Thinking about the end—in both how you want to be remembered and the legacy you leave—is a necessary discipline. Stan Craig provides us with a **transgenerational guide to the excellent stewardship of life.**"

> —DAN DUMAS
> *Pastor, Eastside Community Church*
> *Senior Vice President*
> *The Southern Baptist Theological Seminary*

"This book will change your life and your legacy. Your loved ones will be in a better place when you go to your resting place if you get (or are given) this book and follow its advice."

> —BRIAN KLUTH
> *Pastor, Bestselling author of Because You Are Loved CHRISTIAN LEGACY ORGANIZER and 40 Day Journey to a More Generous Life*

"Every **pastor** ought to know how to provide specific guidance with end of life issues by being able to discuss hospitalization, the required Durable Powers of Attorney, burial, cremation, planned funerals and generosity *ForeTalk* **is the place to find what you and your folks need to know in a single easy to read and apply guidebook**.

— RUSTY ELLISON
*Senior Pastor*
*Walnut Street Baptist Church*

"In *ForeTalk* Stan Craig **combines the heart of a pastor with the acumen of a financial professional,** and has given us the best resource I know of on legacy and end-of-life decisions. **Stan has done a service for us all in this book. Every adult needs to read** *ForeTalk*."

— DR. JASON ALLEN
*President*
*Midwestern Baptist Seminary*

"*ForeTalk* teaches how to manage life effectively, efficiently and on purpose. **It is a must-read for every home and family and should be in the libraries of counselors, ministers, and attorneys.** This book will become required reading in our network for all the couples who come our way."

— DON R. "DICK" IVEY, PhD
*CEO*
*TDIB Associates, LLC*

"*ForeTalk* meets a need that most everyone we know failed to fulfill because, as *ForeTalk* says, "there was no help, no experience, no learning curve." We believe every pastor, every church and Christian foundation or organization can benefit by *ForeTalk* and having a **ForeTalk Seminar.**

Read *ForeTalk*. **You will be informed, your family strengthened and your future more secure.**"

— DAN and ANGELA BIGGS
*Executive Directors*
*Connect Financial Ministries*

"*ForeTalk* opens doors for all of us to have the serious, meaningful conversations that matter. Insurance is often one of those conversations. *ForeTalk* introduces insurance protection and much more of what we need to know and why. Plus, read *ForeTalk*; share it; complete your own checklist. Your family will be glad for the time you gave and the conversations you shared."

— KENTON HAYES
*Founder and President*
*Hayes, Utley and Hedgspeth Insurance*

"Business leaders as well as churches and individuals will benefit from *ForeTalk.* Anticipating change in planning for the future is not only smart; it is a requirement to be an effective leader. *ForeTalk* **tackles the tough questions and offers practical and applicable answers that will help everyone plan for the future.**

— STEVE STEVENSON
*President*
*Comdata Corporation*

**The ForeTalk Seminar attendees are unanimous …**
*Talking about expected events seems only to work for the things we believe will be enjoyable. Perhaps that is why we put off talking about difficult topics. But it is precisely the conversations about difficult topics that take away much of the difficulty. Here is how to get it done.*

"The **ForeTalk Seminar** will help you find exactly how to talk to your spouse, your family, your attorney and other professionals about your most meaningful experiences in life and how to make them even more meaningful to your family. It has made a difference for us now and will in our future."

— MR. & MRS. REX SLECHTER

"**S**o much has changed in the last 10 years in medicine, healthcare, estate planning…we were shocked at how much we did not know and how little it took for us to get the comfort and peace of mind we needed. Everyone benefits from *ForeTalk*."

— MR. & MRS. BUD FEKETE

"**OK,** let's do it again! I am still surprised at what we found out and want to attend the next seminar and bring my son and his family. We need to think together as a family and plan together. I have seen the pain in families who ignored foretalk. That is not us, thanks to *ForeTalk*."

— MR. & MRS. DICK AYLER

"**W**hen my mother passed away, everything was put on me with no help. It was a very sad time. Now my family will not have to go through that because of the **ForeTalk Seminar.** Thanks so much."

— MRS. HOLLY POWELL

"**W**ow, expectations were high but far exceeded. It was a great time with fun but serious stuff. I will use my checklist and begin tonight with my Letter of Gratitude. It will all get done now that I know what it all means. I am so glad we were here."

— MRS. MARILEE MILLER

"**T**his is a message we all need to hear. Everyone benefits. Gratitude and generosity, confidence and security for the future are just a few of the benefits from *ForeTalk*. Stan is one of our favorite speakers. He makes serious stuff easy to understand and even funny. His message touches the audience with both tears and encouragement for a life well lived."

— VICKY DAUGHERTY
*Oasis (Older Adults Still In Service)*

# ACKNOWLEDGMENTS

*ForeTalk* was written to help all of us follow Biblical wisdom as we approach the end of life. While the information in *ForeTalk* will be helpful to every family, it was written specifically to Christian families, those who acknowledge the Lordship of Jesus Christ; that's where wisdom truly begins. The first acknowledgment is to Him who gave us grace upon grace so that we could truly live life to the fullest, both here and in eternity.

- To my dear wife, Gloria, who edited, rewrote, corrected and gave fresh ideas and insight on every page of this book. Her patience, understanding and love were confirmed in every writing session. She was tireless in her work, continuous in her support…

- To my family, who edited, offered suggestions and freely expressed their love over the years and first made us sensitive to the wisdom of planning…

- To my friend and pastor, Rusty Ellison, Senior Pastor of Walnut Street Baptist Church, who gave most welcome encouragement to the *ForeTalk* Seminars and this book…

- To Lee Richardson, my friend, attorney and specialist in elder law, who shared his knowledge and edited the chapters specifically relating to legal questions…

- To Barry Allen and Laurie Valentine of the Kentucky Baptist Foundation who participated in every *ForeTalk* seminar with knowledge and skill, and assisted the work of creating this book with their kind and gracious words…

- To Brian Kluth, whose demonstrated faith and commitment to teaching and practicing generosity inspired this work from its inception…

- To Leana Santana, my book designer, whose creativity brought this book to life and whose talent and guidance is apparent from the cover to the final copy…

- To the members of Walnut Street Baptist Church and Walnut Street Foundation, to the hundreds who turned out to attend the *ForeTalk* seminars…

- And to you who read *ForeTalk* and share it with members of your family and others who need to know how to prepare for the one event in our lives that all of us know will occur…

My deepest gratitude for your confidence and trust and a prayer that God will bless this resource in ways that will not only strengthen families for decades to come but will also bless the work of His kingdom.

*Stan Craig*
*Louisville*
*February 2013*

> Give in to God, come to terms with him and everything will turn out just fine. Let him tell you what to do; take his words to heart. Come back to God Almighty and he'll rebuild your life. Clean house of everything evil. Relax your grip on your money and abandon your gold-plated luxury. God Almighty will be your treasure, more wealth than you can imagine.
>
> JOB 22:21-25

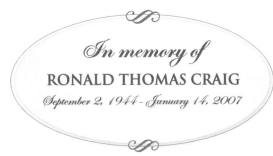

*In memory of*
**RONALD THOMAS CRAIG**
*September 2, 1944 - January 14, 2007*

# Table of Contents

Welcome to *ForeTalk*. Here is what to expect.

# ForeTalk:
# The Seven
# Critical Conversations

INTRODUCTION

## Living in the Season of Now

**So teach us to number our days that we might apply our hearts to wisdom.** PSALM 90:12

There is a new word for you to add to your vocabulary: foretalk—(fohr-tawk) n. 1. a conversation about an expected event 2. the act of discussing an upcoming event or experience. *Foretalk* is about life affirmation. There are seven critical conversations that are about planning—not only for the end of life (expected or unexpected), but about life itself. All of our lives will come to an end. This is an expected event! You can simply drift without direction, or you can discuss, prepare and plan by having these seven critical conversations. Life goes on—even when yours doesn't.

Your birth was more than likely anticipated and prepared for. It was talked about; there was foretalk. Birthdays, anniversaries, marriages are all very common occasions that call for foretalk. But at times the more serious the subject, the more we fail to have the conversation. **Planning for tomorrow but believing tomorrow will never come is contradictory. All expect to get older but act as if the end of life will never occur. Yet, also know, it can end anytime, in a fraction of a second.** That is why personally, legally, financially, you cannot afford to skip foretalk when it comes to…

- writing a will
- selecting someone to act on your behalf
- hospitalization
- serious illness
- incapacity
- funeral planning
- paying last expenses
- legacy gifts and generosity
- expressing your love and concern for those people and causes dear to you

There are several reasons many put off end-of-life discussions:

- We have questions but no answers.
- The subject is disturbing to us or others.
- It is forced on us by circumstance and we are caught off guard.
- We feel ill-equipped to handle the conversation.
- No one ever discussed the topic with us; there was no learning curve.
- There may be some personal pain relevant to the conversation.
- The topic seems so far off that a conversation can be easily and safely delayed.
- We are afraid of the topic.

Have you ever thought, "We need to talk," but avoided the discussion? It is easy to do and, sadly, responsible for so much pain. To have worked hard, created a life of meaning, then to fail to affirm your own beliefs and wishes for those most important to you can be a heart-wrenching tragedy.

But not for you or your family. You are now on your way to living with a sense of personal satisfaction and peace because you are ready to begin *ForeTalk*. These seven critical conversations will prepare you and those you care about most for the end of life whenever it might come.

*ForeTalk* combines Biblical wisdom and contemporary insight to create the conver-

sations you must have. *ForeTalk* **is about life affirmation. It is about living with peace and confidence in a future where anticipation becomes preparation.**

# How this book is organized

Each chapter will cover a specific topic. The subject matter is designed to be a guide, easy to read, informative, and helpful. However, every topic will require a much more detailed and personal review. **The goal of** *ForeTalk* **is to make you aware of the decisions you need to make now, or help someone else make**—writing a will, completing a Durable Power of Attorney for Health Care, a Durable Power of Attorney for Finances, perhaps a Living Will. There is also significant related information to directly benefit you and your loved ones now. Start writing notes in the space provided. Write whatever comes to mind; these are your notes and will save you time in review. Mark up the text. This is your book. Use it!

At the beginning of each chapter, you will find an outline of the major topics covered in the chapter. It begins with **A Look Ahead**.

At the end of each chapter is a special section called **Afterthought**. This section is designed to help you take care of tomorrow today by putting into practice what you have learned in the chapter.

In the **Afterthought** section, you will find three icons:

 The first icon tells you
*what the law requires.*

 The second icon tells you
*what the law means to you.*

 The third icon tells you
*what you need to do now*
to make sure you and your
family are prepared to act on
the information.

Following **Afterthought** is **Follow-up**. Now that you know what to do, it is time to do it. **Follow-up** will provide a checklist to take the next steps. Knowing what to do is one thing; doing it is another.

> **The wisdom of the wise
> keeps life on track;
> the foolishness of fools
> lands them in the ditch.**
>
> PROVERBS 14:8

# Now, let's begin...

# Why Conversation Is Critical Now

## CHAPTER ONE

The good acquire a taste for helpful conversation; bullies push and shove their way through life. Careful words make for a careful life; careless talk may ruin everything.  PROVERBS 13:2-3

*"This is why I loved support groups so much. If people thought you were dying, they gave you their full attention. If this was the last time they saw you, they really saw you. People listened instead of just waiting for their turn to speak. And when they spoke, they weren't telling you a story. When the two of you talked, you were building something, and afterward you were both different than before." – Chuck Palschiuk*

*Some people love surprises. For others they are most unfortunate. Here are some of those times when foretalk was needed but did not occur, and then...*

• *Gerry was rushed to the hospital. His emergency surgery for a ruptured gallbladder came too late. Gerry survived the surgery, but did not regain consciousness. He was kept alive by a breathing machine and an intravenous drip. His wife was convinced this was not what he would have wanted, but, without a Living Will and specific directions, family members were at a loss over what to do.*

• *Marge had been visiting her son, Collin, in Pennsylvania when she was killed in an auto accident. Collin wanted her to be cremated and her ashes scattered there—close to him. However, Marge's husband, Collin's stepdad, had bought side-by-side crypts in Florida, his and Marge's home for the last 8 years. Collin and Marge's bereaved husband argued over the decision and what Marge*

4

*would have wanted. No one knew for certain because Marge had not written down her wishes. Her son wanted one thing and her husband wanted something else. The debate began, creating winners and losers.*

- *The retirement facility was top-ranked and beautiful with every service for residents. Virginia and Ed sold their home of 40 years and moved into one of the beautiful two-bedroom apartments. An endowment of $100,000 deposited with the facility lowered the monthly rent substantially, offering a decided advantage in cash outlay as the years passed. But less than 2 months after moving in, Virginia died unexpectedly; Ed passed away 6 weeks later. The endowment will be returned to the family only under the terms of the contract that specified a 10-year payout—a long time to wait. Failing to discuss documents with their family before signing resulted in a frustrating surprise.*

- *The most valuable thing Jim could leave his two daughters was equal shares in his house. He knew he could write his own will and he did. Years later his oldest daughter was divorced and her daughter, his granddaughter, was living a lifestyle he did not want his assets to support. So Jim wrote a note to remove her from his will. His handwriting was not always legible and his intentions were unclear. The sisters stopped talking to each other. The house was locked in a court dispute.*

There are hundreds of stories just like these that, in hindsight, never needed to occur. All it would have taken was a bit of forethought and "foretalk."

*What is foretalk? It is thinking ahead **and** talking.*
*It is taking many of the uncertainties out of the future.*
*ForeTalk means addressing these life-affirming decisions*
*before they become personal and hard-to-resolve family issues:*

- Are there laws specifically applied to me as I get older?
- What is elder law?
- What do I need to know about charitable gifts?
- What property or personal items are important to my children, grandchildren, family members and special friends?
- Are there investment options for me that may provide more income for me and/or my heirs?
- Who are my trusted advisors?
- Who will speak for me if I am incapacitated?
- What is hospice?
- What does "do not resuscitate" mean?
- Do I really need a will?
- How often should I update it?
- What if I have no heirs?
- How will state law and tax codes impact my family after my death?
- What about being an organ donor— is that always appropriate?
- Who will be the guardian of my dependent children and/or my other dependents?
- Who will care for my pets?
- What is the best way of letting my family know my wishes after my death?
- What will become of my property and possessions that are important to me?
- What about a prepaid funeral? Is that a wise decision?
- Is cremation an option? What will become of the ashes? How do my loved ones feel about that?
- Where will I be buried? Do I want a funeral service or memorial service?
- Are there local or family traditions or expectations to fulfill?

Many of these questions need your response now, in writing and, in some cases, made binding by legal documents. You should understand and discuss the importance of the key documents you must complete for your family while you can.

# A personal story

*Ron was 61, broke, and in pain from being injured in an auto accident two years earlier. He was expecting an insurance settlement by year end to compensate for his permanent injuries. While the family was celebrating Thanksgiving, he sat alone in his favorite chair in front of the TV watching, but not listening to, the football game. As his family joined him in the living room, he slowly stood and asked his brothers to come to his bedroom and chat for a minute. He was ashen, weak, out of breath and had all-too-frequent serious coughing spasms. Closing the bedroom door, he unbuttoned his shirt revealing dark blotches all across his chest. Ron was a heavy smoker and he was scared.*

*The next day his brothers took him to the hospital emergency room. The diagnosis was lung cancer, advanced stage. He was admitted and aggressive treatment was started. He had to make a "do not resuscitate" decision while being treated for cancer. His family had to help him prepare his will while making every attempt to be encouraging about his recovery. Legal documents had to be created while he was weakened from the aggressive treatment prescribed by his team of physicians. Instead of the comfort of having made these decisions prior to his illness, he began to fear he had waited too long to begin his treatment and end-of-life planning. He was right. Ron never left the hospital. On January 14 he passed away. The insurance settlement, which he had willed to his ex-wife, created a sizable estate. It was to be paid three months after his death—and it was contested.*

*Adopted children whom he had not heard from in years, from a marriage 25 years in the past and unknown to the*

*rest of his family, claimed his assets. They asserted that when Ron wrote his will in the hospital, he was not mentally capable of making decisions. They claimed he was incompetent because of the effects of his treatment and was under undue influence from family members. It took two years for the court to render a final decision. The claims were denied. Two years of fees and expenses were taken from his insurance settlement before the proceeds of his estate could be paid. In the meantime, his beneficiary, the ex-wife with whom he had reunited, was diagnosed with pancreatic cancer. The lawsuit had created years of unnecessary pain and sadness for everyone.*

Had Ron known what was ahead, he wouldn't have waited to complete the documents he needed for the sake of his loved ones. Ron was my brother. As a result of his death, I became personally aware of the need for conversation about events we know will occur before they occur—"foretalk."[1]

In hindsight, I could have encouraged Ron to do the things we all need to do: to understand that these are not fearful decisions but life affirming decisions—positive, take-charge acts of kindness and blessing. How could I have started such a conversation? Some suggestions are in this book.

# Foretalk is better than hindsight

Harriet Beecher Stowe said, "The bitterest tears shed over graves are for words left unsaid and deeds left undone."[2] This book will help you prevent those bitter tears by understanding the benefits of foretalk.

Every 3.6 seconds another man or woman passes away without taking the most basic steps to help their family cope with the loss and continuing pain. Failing to **talk** now—**before** you or your loved ones are unable to—can bring about misery and create animosity and distrust among family members for generations to come. Why not solve end-of-life issues before they arrive? *ForeTalk* is designed to make the complicated easy to understand and simple to carry out.

## *Do any of these excuses sound familiar to you?*

- "It's too complicated; I don't know anything about that stuff."
- "There are too many people taking advantage of folks like me."
- "I'm not ready to talk about dying; it's hard enough living."

- "I don't want to talk about it right now!"
- "This just isn't the right time; I'll do something later."
- "None of this applies to me; I don't have enough money or stuff to worry about."
- "Somebody else can take care of all that after I'm gone."
- "I did all this a few years back. I think that should do it. I'm done."

Divorce, blended families, existing medical conditions, and fear of the unknown may be unspoken reasons for "putting it off" until later. No one wants to upset loved ones by forcing the discussion on those who say, "Not right now; we can do it later."

Whatever reasons may come to mind, there are none good enough to put off this discussion. Not having foretalk now may deny your loved ones the protection and peace of mind every family deserves. **A startling 70% of those who read this book do not have a will or the other significant documents we all need.** And of those who do have a will, many are outdated. You, your spouse, perhaps your parents and your adult children need to talk.

It's no accident that the symbol on the cover of this book is a tree going through the four seasons of change with a clock representing the ticking away of the seconds, minutes and hours of every day. Writers and poets have suggested that our lives go through four seasons. The ticking clock reminds us that we never know when we are in our final season.

NOTES

The passing of time brings unexpected or age-related difficulties that can make discussions impossible. Although everyone is "busy," we must take the time now, before time is gone.

There are basic documents that can solve a wide range of future problems and resolve some of the frustrations that may face your family.

You sign many documents in your life. However, **the documents you sign regarding the later years of your life may be some of the most important ones you will ever sign.**

## *Significant benefits from talking now!*

- Save thousands of dollars in fees and expenses.
- Spare loved ones tragic and needless heartache.
- Ensure your expressions of concern are understood.
- Keep predators and thieves out of your savings and your family's future financial health.
- Avoid costly and painful mistakes.
- Remove potential fear and doubt from your family's future today
- Find ways your current investments can benefit you now as well as provide for your heirs.

- Enjoy the peace of mind that comes from knowing you have done your best to solve any future problems that could come from an accident, illness or other incapacitating, life-threatening experience.

You cannot predict what tomorrow may bring. Every time you look at the clock, remember—time is not on your side.

Answers to most of your questions are in the chapters that follow. You will find a straight-forward presentation with a simple check-list of actions at the end of each chapter. The documents essential to end-of-life planning are described: ideas, suggestions and the guidance you and your family need now are here. The website **www.ForeTalkSeminar. com** will keep the information up-to-date as laws change and new questions and issues arise.

Critical conversations with your spouse, children and family members about what is meaningful to all of you may be one of the biggest blessings this book can provide. *ForeTalk* will help you find the occasion to talk with your loved ones about one of the most serious questions in life: "How do I make my life count now and in the future?" This is not about dying; it's about affirming your life in the decisions you make today.

You do not want to be remembered for your tragic neglect—your loved ones going through financial and personal disarray because you left them without a plan or direction. You would rather be thought of with love and appreciation—your family and loved ones grateful for the time, the care and compassion you gave to keep them from the helplessness they would experience without your guidance.

It is my prayer that, as you consider these life-affirming decisions, you will be prepared and grateful for the foretalk you had to resolve potential issues long before they could cause pain and difficulties for your family.

**This is an exercise to savor, anticipate and learn from. You may be surprised to discover how enjoyable foretalk can be.**

*Foretalk is always better
than hindsight!*

*Make a great
LAST impression by taking care
of tomorrow today.*

# Can we talk?

When and how do you talk about matters relating to the end of life, the serious and deep conversations? How do you begin?

> Dear friend, pay close attention to this, my wisdom: listen closely to the way I see it. Then you will acquire a taste for good sense; what I tell you will keep you out of trouble.
>
> PROVERBS 5: 1-2

Have you ever noticed that there are people for whom conversation seems to come easy? In fact, there are those who seem to be talking all the time.

*Gloria and Carol, two friends who had not seen each other for years, were renewing their friendship by visiting over lunch.*

*Carol noticed the large diamond ring on Gloria's finger and commented, "My, what a beautiful ring and such a large diamond."*

*Gloria replied, "Yes, it is beautiful, isn't it? But sadly, it came with the Grayson curse."*

*"What's the Grayson curse?" asked Carol.*

*Gloria said quietly, "Mr. Grayson!"*

Social theorists suggest there are five levels of conversation. The first level is the casual conversation like Gloria and Carol's chat. The fifth level is serious and deep. This is the most meaningful type of conversation—and the one seldom practiced.

## A look ahead

- **The #1 reason to have the seven critical conversations now**
- **When and how to begin and what to say**
- **How to get started:** *The Personal Property Inventory*

The benefits of *ForeTalk* begin with conversation that can keep trouble away from the door. Conversation is important. Many of us don't know what we are thinking until we hear ourselves say it.

**You and your spouse or significant other, your parents or children and your family members need to be able to talk about life planning and begin making these life-affirming decisions.**

Avoiding any awareness of the reality of death is a goal of much of our society. Funerals are disappearing and are being replaced with memorial services. The body of a deceased loved one is often hidden and never seen by children or adults. And when a funeral is held there is either a closed casket or no casket at all. So how do you begin these important conversations?

When and how do you talk about matters relating to the end of life, the serious and deep conversations? How do you begin?

Bob Harrington, the chaplain of Bourbon Street, would always get a laugh when he asked, "How many of you call up your friends and invite them over for MoonPies and an RC Cola to discuss who's going to die next? You want to kill a party? Just make that the topic of conversation. Man, I want to go to heaven; I just don't want to be on the next bus."

Not even a MoonPie or RC Cola (Southern delicacies) can make the topic palatable for some.

These seven critical conversations are simple enough to be discussed in a single setting. They are also detailed enough that it may take some time to discuss and set a plan of action in place. The most important thing is to get started and that's what we are going to do next. Death is an unwelcome intruder no matter what the season. But our faith and preparation can help us lessen and sometimes even remove its sting.

> ### *"All my possessions for a moment of time."*
> *– Elizabeth I,*
> *Queen of England, d. 1603*

# The #1 reason to have the seven critical conversations now

**End-of-life planning has one primary purpose: to provide peace of mind for you and those you love—now and when the inevitable end-of-life occurs.** Parents would do anything to save and protect the lives of their children. Children, too, when seeing danger for their parents, would be quick to get them out of harm's way. Let me be clear—parents and children forfeit peace of mind and security when these discussions are ignored, put off, or forgotten.

> The gossip of bad people gets them into trouble; the conversation of the good keeps them out of it. PROVERBS 12:13

If all of your family were in a van driving along the highway and you saw a semi-truck racing toward you at high speed in your lane of traffic, you would take careful control of the van and get it out of the way as quickly and as safely as possible. *There is a semi coming your way. The driver is death.* No matter your skill or strength, a collision is coming. When the family is unprepared—no foretalk, no life plan, few or no necessary documents in place—the devastation death brings can have heart-breaking and lasting consequences. Take the wheel. Take charge. Protect your family.

There are times when death is a welcome friend. A debilitating illness can sap the strength both physically and mentally. In those cases, death is often welcomed when, easily and quietly, we go to sleep to wake in a place we can only imagine. But even then, without planning, difficult times may lie ahead for our families.

> *It pays to plan ahead. It wasn't raining when Noah built the ark.*

Having a plan in place not only protects your family, but it will provide peace of mind for everyone concerned. Knowing that these matters have already been thought through in a positive, proactive manner can reduce stress and end anxious nights for everyone involved.

**Let's suppose that your spouse, significant other, or parents are not willing to have these critical conversations.** Let's suppose they say, "I don't want to talk about this now." What do you do? Turn to the Follow-up section at the end of this chapter and review the section called "Family Matters." There you will find family history and legacy questions to get you started. After a time of what can be an enjoyable and interesting conversation, it should to be much easier to say, "While we're talking, we ought to talk about end-of-life matters." Talking about our memories is fun and informative, but talking about the future is critical.

# When and how to begin and what to say

## 1 When an acquaintance is ill

In today's connected world of computers, smart phones, iPads, and social networking, we are all more aware than ever of the health of our friends and acquaintances. Whenever we hear of the health challenges that others are facing, it offers an ideal time to say, "You know, we ought to talk about our wills and estate plans while we're both healthy."

## 2 When someone you know has died

Death is always unsettling, especially when it takes away a friend or family member. Even the death of a public figure, celebrity or world leader makes us aware of the brevity of life. "We need to talk about our wills and powers of attorney while we are thinking about it."

## 3 When someone you know is facing a life-threatening illness

Any serious illness among our friends reminds us all of our mortality. It makes it much easier to say, "You just never know when something like this is going to happen. This might be our wake-up call to get our own life planning done. We ought to talk about our will, visit our attorney, review our plans, and talk about powers of attorney and our funeral planning."

NOTES

## 4  When a major life event takes place

There are many major events in our lives that are happy and significant occasions. Those happy times are appropriate for discussing future issues. The birth of a child, graduation, marriage, retirement, wedding anniversary, move to a new home are all ideal occasions to talk about the future. "Things change so fast, don't they? I think we should take the time to talk about our wills, powers of attorney and other documents while we're thinking about it."

## 5  When a long vacation or overseas trip is planned

A friend of ours was taking a group of school-aged teens on a two-week tour of Europe. This made him consider reviewing his will and other necessary documents. (Traveling with teenagers can prompt that reaction.) Travel risk is everywhere and makes discussing life planning relevant to the most fearless as well as the most fearful. "Before we leave, we need to have a serious talk about our planning and make sure all of our documents are up to date."

## 6  When visiting the doctor for your own needs and concerns

There are often unspoken concerns when a potential life-threatening illness comes into our lives. Anxiety and needless stress can result from failing to discuss the possible outcome. An ideal time for foretalk is following a doctor's visit. Turn off the television or computer, put down the newspaper, and begin the conversation that must take place. "You know, we still have some things we need to talk about as we go through this."

## 7  When we read about a disaster or event in which unexpected death occurred

The newspaper, TV, and online news are quick to report deaths and tragedy. "If it bleeds, it reads" is the standard in effect in every form of media. The reason is simple. We pay attention to a report of loss of life— from the horrific numbers of lives lost in floods or earthquakes anywhere in the world to local reports of serious injuries or death. Human-interest stories touch our lives. They also call attention to our own limited lifespans. "Did you read the news today? It reminded me that we need to get prepared in case something like that were to happen to us."

**Don't be concerned if you find it difficult to get the conversation started. Even physicians have difficulty when it comes to discussing the topic.** A study at the University of Washington in Seattle found that even though they were in a conference with the family while the family member was in intensive care, physicians missed opportunities to talk about the end of life 29% of the time. No one should feel distress over missing past opportunities when even professionals can miss the occasion for serious conversation.

# How to get started
## What documents are helpful?

How do you start a process that most assume will be painful? One way is to begin with the least threatening and yet one of the most important documents you will create: the Personal Property Inventory.

## The Personal Property Inventory

Start with the Personal Property Inventory (PPI) at the end of this chapter and any documents and/or account statements showing your assets: bank accounts, both savings and checking; annuities and insurance policies, indicating their values and policy numbers; certificates of deposit; mutual funds; and stocks, bonds or treasury notes that may be held at a brokerage house or in a safe deposit box. List all IRA accounts or retirement or pension accounts by name and account number along with their current values. List all the real estate owned or partially owned, and any business ventures or partnerships that may be in existence. List all your valuable items, cars, boats, or other recreational equipment. Art, jewelry, and any family heirlooms should also be listed. You may be surprised to see how much you actually own.

You should determine the ownership of any real estate, bank accounts, and personal property—not including insurance policies or annuities. Insurance policies and annuities have a beneficiary listed, which will take care of their disposition.

In many cases, property and bank accounts are held jointly with a spouse or adult child. Property held in joint ownership usually is stated as Joint Ownership with Right of Survivorship (JOWROS). That means that when one of the owners dies, the surviving owner will own 100% of the property. Be aware, though, that being listed as co-owner of a bank account could affect eligibility for public benefit programs such as Medicaid. The transfer of a home, car, or securities normally requires the signature of all the owners, and the loss of capacity of one owner can prevent the sale or transfer of the property.

It is also important to write down the location of these assets. Where are the insurance policies, bank and retirement account statements? It is not uncommon to miss assets, even significant ones, simply because no one knew they existed, or they knew they existed but couldn't find any proof of their ownership or their location.

**Most state laws say that checking and savings accounts, brokerage accounts, and mutual fund accounts that have three years of inactivity and an unknown address officially become abandoned property.**

There are literally hundreds of millions of dollars lost to family, friends and charities because someone didn't list his or her assets and where to find them.

*"When people talk, listen completely. Most people never listen."*
— *Ernest Hemingway*

# One of the best days of my life

There was a time when families actually sat down and ate meals together, talked about each other's thoughts, hopes and dreams. Remember? Those days are gone. Today many families seldom sit down to a meal together except at a restaurant. Have you noticed how few couples or families speak to each other even at a restaurant? Electronic games and texting have taken children out of conversation and cell phones with Internet access have removed the adults. No one speaks. **It is a sad result of our technology that, while we have increasingly effective ways of communicating, we actually talk less and less.** Perhaps that's why having a serious conversation about a meaningful topic can be difficult and yet so rewarding.

*Brian, a 46-year-old father of four, was visiting his dad on his father's 74th birthday. Late that afternoon, Brian and his dad drove to the local coffee shop to chat about the day. What would have been a typical 15-minute visit turned into a two-hour conversation. Brian had been to a ForeTalk Seminar the weekend before and remembered what he had learned about how to start a meaningful conversation (see pg. 21). He asked his father, "Dad, what's the first birthday you remember as a child?" Soon they were both enjoying conversation about birthdays past and birthdays to come. Brian told his dad that he was taking seriously the need for life planning and discussing end-of-life issues with his wife. Then he said, "Dad, have you given any thought to life planning and end-of-life matters? It's something we've never discussed." For the next hour father and son had serious conversations about the people they love the most and what they were doing and needed to do to protect them from unnecessary worry.*

*As they stood to leave, Brian reached over and gave his dad a hug. As they embraced, his father said, "You know what, Son? This is one of my best birthdays."*

*Brian said, "Dad, I'm glad we can talk about things that really matter."*

There was more to talk about. That night when they returned home, dad and mom, son and wife began foretalk. They discussed the importance of having wills and durable powers of attorney and created plans of action.

> **"There isn't much better in this life than finding a way to spend a few hours in conversation with people you respect and love. You have to carve this time out of your life because you aren't really living without it."**
> **— Anonymous**

# Afterthought

There are legal complications that will directly affect you if you don't have these critical conversations with your loved ones. As you may know, you already have a will written for you by your state. It may not be to your liking, so, right now, schedule your deadline for having a serious conversation with your family, spouse, parents and/or children.

 Start getting references for an attorney. Download any legal information from your state regarding end-of-life issues. Review online documents and begin to think seriously about your situation.

 Begin this process with the end in mind. It is not a difficult process but it will take time. The result and the peace of mind you will experience are benefits that are incalculable now and will be even more valuable when the documents are called for.

 Being organized is essential when a death occurs. Take time now to turn to the final chapter and see all that is required (p. 164). Review the documents, consider who your trusted advisors are and prepare to make the most of the tools and resources of *ForeTalk*.

## PRAYER

*Heavenly Father,* You prepared everything necessary for all our needs, our world and all that is in it. You even planned for our Savior to come and rescue us from our own sin, our struggles with death and heartache. Thank You, Father, for Your preparation. Help us to follow Your lead and to express our gratitude that death is not the final chapter in our lives but the opening chapter in an entirely new part of Your plan for us. Grant that we may begin our planning so that our loved ones will be able to rejoice in our preparation as we rejoice in Yours. We ask this in the name of Him Who prepared the way for all of us and Who was, in the very beginning, Your loving plan. Bless all who read these words and prepare for a future in Your presence. AMEN

# Follow-up

## I. FAMILY MATTERS— CONVERSATION STARTERS

The conversation starters that follow are designed to open the door to more serious conversation. However, you will also find them helpful in getting to know more about the people in your life. Far too often, people pass away without our ever knowing as much about them as we would have liked. Sometimes we are amazed at how little we know about someone who was very dear to us. Why didn't we talk more? Why didn't we ask more questions? Don't miss the opportunity for conversation. (You might want to take notes. There are tidbits of information you can glean that one day will delight a grandchild or great grandchild.)

**Recording these conversations (either video or audio) can create a precious family artifact to treasure. Modern technology can make old-fashioned conversation endure for generations.**

- Where were you born?

- What schools did you attend and what do you remember the most about attending school?

- What were your favorite activities or pastimes as a child?

- Who were your friends in childhood and what do you remember most about them?

- What chores did you do while growing up? Were you paid for doing them or did you receive an allowance? If so, how much?

- Do you recall special family holidays or vacations?

- Did you have any hobbies or collections?

- Did you learn a language or how to play an instrument?

- What was one of your happiest times as a child?

- What did you want to be when you grew up?

- Do you remember early boyfriends or girlfriends?

- What do you recall about church, Sunday School or Bible study, Vacation Bible School?

- Who was your favorite relative as you were growing up?

- Did you have a favorite teacher in school or a favorite subject?

- What grades did you get in grade school, high school and/or college? Did they ever change over time? Why?

- Did you have any nicknames while growing up? What were they?

- What did you call your grandparents as you were growing up?

- Do you remember any pets you had as a child?

- Did your family ever talk about money?

- What did you learn about money?

- What's the first job you recall that you enjoyed?

- How did you come to your career or job choice?

- Were there any influential books, movies, or television shows that you recall?

- What's the most exciting trip you've ever taken?

- What's the most exciting thing you've ever done?

- What do you remember about your family relationships with your mother and dad or brothers and sisters?

- Do you remember any favorite clothes that you were particularly proud of?

- Was there an occasion that was especially meaningful to you, perhaps even more than one?

- Were there any events in your life that were painful or difficult for you? How did you cope with them?

- Who was your first love, first kiss, first serious relationship, first heartbreak?

- Who was the most influential person in your life as a child, in adulthood, and later in life?

- What was the best advice you've ever received?

- What's the origin of your name and how did you select the names of your children?

- As you think about your children or grandchildren, what makes you the most proud about each of them?

- Do you have a favorite song, poem, or book?

- How did you meet your spouse? What attracted you to each other? What do you recall about your dating, courtship, engagement, wedding day, and honeymoon?

- What are your favorite memories of your children? What was the most fun experience and the most frightening experience you can recall?

- Did you ever meet anyone famous?

- Did you attend any memorable sports events, concerts, or performances that were meaningful to you?

- What times in your life do you recall being the happiest?

- What times in your life do you recall feeling sad?

- Are there things in your life you're glad you managed to avoid?

- What do you consider to be your spiritual heritage?

- When were you baptized?

- What churches have you belonged to?

- When have you felt most spiritually alive?

- Are there favorite photos that you remember or have on display? Please show them to me.

- What are some of the most important lessons you've learned over your lifetime?

- What are some of the things you would still like to do?

*"Most conversations are simply monologues delivered in the presence of the witness." – Margaret Miller*

# II. GETTING TO THE SERIOUS QUESTIONS

There is a sense of satisfaction in asking and answering life's difficult questions, especially those regarding the end of life. Here are transitions to begin talking about them.

- Now that we have some time to chat, can I ask you for some help? I have been reading that everyone needs to have a will, a Durable Power of Attorney for Finances, a Durable Power of Attorney for Health Care and a Living Will. Can we talk about that?

- Do you have a will?

- When was the last time your will was reviewed? Does it need to be updated?

- Have you appointed someone to act on your behalf in financial matters if you are incapacitated?

- Have you appointed someone to act on your behalf in regard to health care?

- If hospitalized, you need to be sure that you have a Living Will in place. Have you made a Living Will?"

These documents need to be current and must reflect any changes in circumstances and in the current law. They also need to be in a place where they can be found quickly if something were to happen.

# III. PERSONAL PROPERTY INVENTORY

**It begins with your family information.**

*(Add additional pages as needed.)*

| | |
|---|---|
| Full name | |
| Nicknames or other names | |
| Date of birth | Social Security number |
| Place of birth | Citizenship |
| Current address | |
| City and State | Years you lived there |
| Second home address | |
| Marital status | Prior marriage(s) |

## FAMILY INFORMATION

| | |
|---|---|
| Spouse's name | |
| Place of marriage | Date of marriage |
| Date of birth | Social Security number |
| Place of birth | Citizenship |
| Home address | |
| City and State | Years lived there |
| Occupation | Employer |
| Prior marriage(s) | |

### Your Children

| Name | Age | Address |
|---|---|---|
| | | |
| | | |
| | | |
| | | |

Do you want all children to inherit equally?

Should your children precede you in death, do you want their share to go to their spouses, their children (your grandchildren), or to your other surviving children?

| Your Spouse's Children *(your stepchildren)* | | |
|---|---|---|
| Name | Age | Address |
| | | |
| | | |
| | | |
| | | |

Do you want your spouses children to inherit equally?

If your spouses children die before you, do you want their share to go to their spouse, to their children, or to your surviving children?

| Your Grandchildren | | |
|---|---|---|
| Name | Age | Address |
| | | |
| | | |
| | | |
| | | |

| Your Parents | |
|---|---|
| Mother | Living or deceased |
| Father | Living or deceased |

| Stepparents | |
|---|---|
| Mother | Living or deceased |
| Father | Living or deceased |
| Your Spouse's Parents | |
| Mother | Living or deceased |
| Father | Living or deceased |
| Your Brothers and Sisters | |
| Name | Living or deceased |
| Address | |
| Name | Living or deceased |
| Address | |
| Name | Living or deceased |
| Address | |
| Name | Living or deceased |
| Address | |

Are there people you particularly want to exclude from your will? If so, please list them.

Are there any adopted children or children from other marriages who may have a claim on your assets? Are there any stepbrothers or stepsisters or any prior relationships who may have a claim on your assets? If so, please list them.

# ASSETS

For some this can be a very lengthy list. It is advisable that you describe, in some detail, each asset that you wish to be a specific gift. List only those items that you believe are valuable and/or will have meaning for others. In describing these assets, be sure to state their ownership. *(e.g., owned solely by you, owned jointly with your spouse, or owned by your spouse)*

| PERSONAL ASSETS |
| --- |
| Description, Location, Ownership, Current Value |
| Bank account |
| Bank account |
| Bank account |
| Bank account |
| Brokerage account(s) |
| CDs |
| Money market fund(s) |
| Pension account(s) |
| Retirement account(s) |
| 401(k)s or IRAs |
| Mutual fund(s) |
| Savings plan(s) |
| Checking account(s) |
| Online account(s) |
| Bond(s) |
| Stock(s) |
| Deferred compensation(s) |
| Annuities |

## PERSONAL PROPERTY

### Description, Location, Ownership, Current Value

Car(s)

Collectibles

Boat(s)

Painting(s)

Sculpture(s)

Valuable jewelry

Watch(es)

Other collectibles

Significant household item(s)

## REAL ESTATE

### Description, Address, Lender, Balance, Ownership, Value

| | | | | | |
|---|---|---|---|---|---|
| Personal residence | | | | | |
| | | | | | |
| | | | | | |
| Second home | | | | | |
| | | | | | |
| | | | | | |
| Interest/time shares | | | | | |
| | | | | | |
| Vacant lots | | | | | |
| | | | | | |
| Farmland | | | | | |
| | | | | | |
| Investment real estate | | | | | |
| | | | | | |
| | | | | | |
| | | | | | |

## BUSINESS INTERESTS
*(Please list all partnerships, limited partnerships, subchapters, or limited liability corporations in your name or in which you have an interest.)*

### Business, Address, Type, Ownership

| | | | |
|---|---|---|---|
| Intellectual property | | | |
| | | | |
| | | | |

Mortgages or leases

Trusts in which you have an interest

Expected inheritance

Other assets

## INSURANCE POLICIES

Type of Policy, Insurance Company, Cash Value

Automobile insurance

Mortgage insurance

Health insurance

Life insurance

Life insurance (from employer)

| Long term care insurance |
| --- |
| |
| Disability insurance |
| |
| Special health policy |
| |
| Travel insurance *(sometimes included with a credit card)* |
| |
| Burial insurance or prepaid contract |
| |
| Other insurance policies |
| |
| |
| |

This list does not include all of the tangibles or intangibles that are meaningful to you. That's why this next document is extremely important. Whether the previous list is long, short, or contains nothing at all, this next document—your final letter—will be most critical to those who care about you.

# IV. YOUR LETTER OF GRATITUDE

There are very few documents you will write in your lifetime that will have more meaning than this final letter. It doesn't need to be a long letter or address everyone in your life. But it does need to resolve any lingering questions and confirm your affection and love for those closest to you. There may be occasions when you would choose not to write a letter of gratitude. In that case, your will can be your last will and testament and your final letter. But if you choose to write this letter, it can be a meaningful expression of what's most significant and most cherished by you and will be a gracious document to share with your loved ones.

Address it to the most significant people in your life. It doesn't have to be a public letter and can be written to whomever you choose. You may write more than one letter; however, in most cases, writing just one letter simplifies your wishes and thoughts in a succinct and meaningful way. It also means there are no additional letters floating around to be searched for after your death.

## Some thoughts to guide you:

- Address it to specific persons but make it a general letter.

- Begin with the things that you are most grateful for—your accomplishments, what you took pride in, meaningful relationships, beliefs and values that were most significant to you.

- You may also want to mention some of those things that you regret.

- It should be an encouraging letter. Include your hopes and wishes for the people you love the most and for everyone in your family.

- State your confidence in the people who will be reading the letter and in the future they will create.

Perhaps you'll want to give permission to sell or dispose of any of your assets that others may want to hold on to in your memory. You may want to include your confidence in a future life to be joyfully shared. You may also want to express your gratitude for special care or appreciation for significant acts offered on your behalf. Above all, it needs to be personal, loving and helpful to those who will read it. Forgiveness and admiration are appropriate to include as well as your prayers, hopes and wishes for their future. It is no time for anger or recriminations.

This letter should also identify the location of all your important documents as well as those to contact after your death. This may include the executor of your will, your agent under a Durable Power of Attorney for Health Care and for Finances, your attorney, your clergyman and others significant to you and your family. Any final instructions you wish to give your loved ones ought to be included in this letter.

Your letter of gratitude should be placed in your papers along with your will and other significant end-of-life documents.

*"Between the great things we can't do and the little things we won't do, the danger is we shall do nothing at all."*
*— Adolf Monod*

# ❧ LETTER OF GRATITUDE ❧

*Along with your gratitude, you may want to include
any regrets for things left undone, and your best wishes.*

# The FIRST *Critical Conversation:*
# Do We Have A Proper Will and Is It Up-to-Date?

> This is what the Lord says: "Put your house in order, because you are going to die." ISAIAH 38:1 NIV

*"Dying is the most embarrassing thing that can ever happen to you, because someone's got to take care of all your details." – Andy Warhol*

One of the tasks when preparing for a long trip or even a weekend away from home is putting your house in order. But coming home, looking around, realizing all the extra effort before you left was really worth it, is such a pleasure. Another way of putting your house in order is to be sure that when your loved ones get together after your funeral or memorial service, they share the same sense of comfort and well-being because of your preparation.

## A look ahead

- **A will is the way**
- **4 answers to *"Why should I?"***
- **10 estate-planning mistakes**
- **Multiplying a gift**

Following a personal inventory, the simplest way to put your house in order is to create a will. So here's the question: do you have a will? If you have a will, has it been updated in the last three years? How about your parents or in-laws—have their wills been updated? If you and your parents have wills, do you know where they are? Are they easily accessible or in a safe deposit box?

If you and your parents have wills, you are among the minority. The truth is, most people do not have a will. **Over 70% of Americans will die without making any preparation for their families after their death.** That is sad! Making a will is one of the simplest and easiest ways to provide for your family after your death. There may have been a time in America when a will was not needed. That time is long past. Where there is something to dispute, there will be disputes.

34

> *"You own stuff. You will die. Someone will get your stuff."*
> *– Jane Bryant Quinn*

In the book of Genesis, there is the story of Jacob and Esau. Jacob tricks his father into giving him Esau's blessing, his inheritance from their father. Disputes, anger, jealousy, fighting, trickery and loss are still occurring when it comes to discussing inheritance. That doesn't have to be. You can settle it now. Here's how.

# A will is the way

How do you want to be remembered? Your will and estate plan will create a part of your history. It will define your legacy to those you love. *A will is simply a written document stating your wishes for the disposition of your property after your death.* Whatever you own at death is called your estate. Your will is the first document of your "estate plan."

> *"History will be kind to me, for I intend to write it."*
> *– Winston Churchill*

## There are 2 ways to create a will

**1 You may write a will entirely in your own handwriting, signed and dated by you.**

This is called a holographic will. The requirements vary from state to state, but essentially all you need to do is declare this is your Last Will and Testament and write your intentions clearly and legibly. A handwritten will is legal in nearly every state.

**The problem with writing your own will is not knowing how to write one well enough to accomplish your wishes.** Type it and it looks more professional. Typed or printed from a computer also says to the court and attorneys that the will has not been altered. But it is not the appearance that counts. It is the content.

*Dr. Phil McGraw, who hosts his own daily television show, was asked to resolve a dispute between two sisters. Their father had left his house to his younger daughter in his handwritten will. Because the will was handwritten at least 10 years before the father died and was not carefully thought out, it contradicted itself and caused confusion and pain to both sisters. The sisters had not been speaking to each other for years because of the dispute.*

*When Dr. Phil reviewed the 10-year-old document with an attorney who was a guest on the program, he concluded, "I don't know what your daddy actually intended but I do know this. He did not intend for anything that he could've written to so divide his daughters that they actually have ended their relationship. No father wants to leave a legacy like that." Dr. Phil introduced civil and family attorney Areva Martin. "Areva, help me out. This seems to be a really good example of why you need to get a lawyer,*

*because this will—which was written out by (their father)—it contradicts itself top, side and bottom. It's full of inconsistencies and one thing kills another."*

*The attorney replied, "...their dad had a couple of things that he wanted to accomplish in this will, but they are conflicting things, and without a lawyer looking at it and telling him what he could and couldn't do, he created now what is essentially a mess. And we see this happen a lot with inheritances."*

*Two sisters, so upset that they go to court, sue each other over their father's will. Dr. Phil concluded, "...that's why you need a lawyer to write these things. Get a lawyer when it's time to plan an estate."*

*The guest attorney replied, "What we just saw was a will that was 10 years old, and clearly this father's wishes had changed. If only he had had a chance to make those changes, I don't think we would've seen the fight that we've had here today."*

**Can you create a do-it-yourself will with forms from an office supply store or the internet?** Yes. You can use do-it-yourself, fill-in-the-blank forms. These are all legal and helpful, but are not always the best choice. There are better ways to create a will that can withstand the rigors of a legal challenge.

**Here are just a few reasons why you may need and require professional help.** If you…

- are in a second marriage
- are in an unmarried relationship
- have stepchildren
- want to treat your children differently or include someone other than a family member
- own assets or a business that may be hard to divide
- want to make a charitable contribution from your estate
- have property located in more than one state or county
- have any reason to believe your competence could be challenged

Remember, the goal is peace and security. In this day of greed, argument, jealousy, and broken families, writing your own will—without legal counsel—may be a costly mistake.

## 2 The second way is to hire an attorney to draw up a Simple Will.

If you have accumulated any sort of assets, like a boat, car, jewelry, trophies, a collection of any sort—coins, porcelain, hunting rifles, doll collections—or have a bank account, you ought to have a Simple Will. A Simple Will is one that applies only to you. It usually costs less than $500 but ensures that your state's laws are met. The more complicated the estate, the higher the costs. No will is free from all challenges. There is an old saying: "Where there is a will, there is someone waiting to challenge it."

If you are single—you need a well-written will. If you are married—you need a well-written will. If you have children—you need a well-written will. If you have any

NOTES

assets at all, a 401(k) or an IRA, own an interest in any property, have any potential heirs—you need a well-drafted will.

## What is a well-drafted will?

- **It completely addresses the laws of your state.** An attorney understands the ins and outs of your state's laws. The state of Louisiana has made it so difficult to draw up a will that even attorneys need an attorney to draw up their wills.

- **It can list an inventory of your personal property and designates those you wish to receive it.** Everything you own is subject to dispute, from grandpa's old shotgun to mom's wedding ring. Unless you make it clear to whom property goes, a dispute can arise. Maybe you just want to direct a sale of everything and distribute the cash. That's fine as long as you make that clear.

- **Money should be distributed on a percentage basis.** "I leave my spouse 90% of my cash" is much more appropriate than "I leave $125,000 to my spouse." Leaving an exact amount can cause all sorts of grief because you have no idea what may remain after any litigation, claims or fees. Here's what I mean. Suppose you leave $10,000 to each of your three surviving children

and *the remainder* to your spouse. After all the fees and expenses are deducted and all the claims paid, there's only $40,000 left. According to the terms of your will, each of your three children will get $10,000—and so will your spouse.

- **It should include not only those you wish to provide for but should also *exclude* those who may come forward with a claim after your death.** This needs to be very carefully thought out and discussed. If you don't want your nephew driving your BMW or your cousin driving off in your new pick-up truck, then you'd better write it down. Be sure to name those specific people you want to exclude or leave a nominal amount. Do not exclude in general, but be specific. If you don't, someone may come to court after your death and argue that you would have wanted them to have a certain item or sum, but you forgot to put them in the will.

## 4 answers to *"Why should I?"*

If you do not have a will, or your parents do not have a will, get on it! There are four main reasons you should make a will ASAP:

### 1 To ensure your wishes are carried out

**Making a will is one way to be certain that your life's work and assets, built up over the years, are passed on to those you care most about.** You may also indicate those you want to exclude from any share in your property or assets. A will ensures your assets will benefit your family and those you are responsible for.

Most of your life has been spent building up your assets: home, car, insurance policies and other investments. You want those assets to go where you believe they will be appreciated and do the most good. There are often other family members and friends who will have their own ideas. So write it down. Then talk to a competent attorney. In today's litigious society, everything can be challenged. An attorney who specializes in wills and estate planning or elder law will be a wonderful addition to your planning and can make an important difference for your heirs.

## 2 To resolve potential family disputes

> Here's a piece of bad luck I've seen happen:
> A man hoards far more wealth
> than is good for him...
> ECCLESIASTES 5:13

*Jim Wiggins, a 42-year old bachelor welder, was angry. His mother had told him the land that had been in his father's family for as long as she could remember would pass to him. However, in her will written years before, all the land was to go to her spouse, Jim's stepfather, Ralph. After the funeral, Ralph told him that the land was not going to be Jim's—that the land belonged to him and he planned to leave it to Jim's stepbrother. Two days later Jim Wiggins was arrested and charged with murder after he shot and killed both his stepfather and*

*stepbrother in anger over the estate.*

That was an extreme reaction to a tragic situation that perhaps might never have occurred if Jim's mother had only updated her will and stated clearly what belonged to her son and to her husband. There may be times when a will can create anger and dispute. Decisions should be discussed as the will is prepared so there are no surprises when it is read.

> *"Relationships of trust depend on our willingness to look not only to our own interests, but also to the interests of others."*
> — *Peter Harquharsen*

instructions in the will, the executor's job may include gathering all the deceased's property, paying debts, expenses and taxes, and then distributing the remainder to the beneficiaries. He or she may also represent you in court or hire an attorney to do so.

## 3 To choose a person you trust to look after your family and your wishes

> And where there's Right, there'll be Peace and the progeny of Right: quiet lives and endless trust.  ISAIAH 32:17

Your will allows you to choose an executor, a person you believe has your best interests at heart. You will select someone in whom you have confidence and one your survivors will respect. Choosing an executor will be one of the most important decisions you make. He or she will make the decisions regarding all aspects of your will. It is often wise to choose a subsequent or alternate executor should the named executor be unable to fulfill that responsibility. In order to follow the

Remember, you want this process to go as smoothly as possible. You may choose your spouse; you may choose one of your children. But it's generally not wise to name all of your children as co-executors. Not only would this mean they all must agree on every action taken, but they also have to sign all the paperwork. Like many important decisions, it will not be easy. Remember, if you do not choose an executor, the court will appoint someone. **No matter whom you choose as your executor, be sure and tell him or her of the choice you've made.** Too many times an executor is surprised to be chosen. You want to be sure that he or she is willing to serve and to discuss any potential problems that may occur.

## 4 To protect your estate from unnecessary taxation

Taxes are a fact of life. As Americans, we believe in our form of government and pay our taxes. However, there are tax laws designed to allow you to pass your assets on to your heirs without a significant tax burden. This is not tax evasion; it is simply tax planning. Understanding current tax law and being sure that your will takes advantage of all the provisions currently available is an important reason to prepare your will now.

The tax law changes today are too often motivated by political interests and not by logic or reason. As Will Rogers said, "The only difference between death and taxes is that death doesn't get worse every time Congress meets."

# 10 estate-planning mistakes

Here is a list of 10 serious mistakes that too many are making when it comes to wills and estate planning. This list may start you thinking about creating your estate plan.

**1 Thinking you don't need an estate plan**
There are few estates too small to have an estate plan. A will lets your loved ones know how you want your assets distributed. Every adult, regardless of age, should have an estate plan.

**2 Putting off writing or updating your will**
Later may be too late. It is especially important for families with minor children to have a will specifying legal guardians and trustees.

**3 Having a will as your total estate plan**
There are other important parts to an estate plan besides a will. Many of the forms in this book will be vital to help you ensure your family's welfare.

NOTES

## 4 Underestimating the size of your estate

Your estate is probably worth more than you think. Have you considered your life insurance, appreciated value of your home and property, a potential inheritance, your retirement plans? Accurate values make a big difference in estate planning.

## 5 Assuming that leaving your estate to your spouse or having all your assets in joint ownership is a complete estate plan

For some this may be a good plan; for others it might be the wrong thing to do. Poor planning can result in substantial and unnecessary federal estate taxes or probate expense upon the death of the surviving spouse. Check with your attorney.

## 6 Not understanding estate and gift taxes

These taxes may be considerably reduced or avoided with proper planning.

## 7 Not using annual gift tax exclusion

This is a good way to enjoy sharing your estate with loved ones and individuals now. It may also help reduce future estate taxes. (As of 2010 you can give $13,000 per person or $26,000 per couple.)

## 8 Keeping life insurance in your estate

Life insurance will be considered part of your taxable estate for federal tax purposes unless you take steps to avoid this potential tax liability.

## 9 Failing to keep good records

All of your assets, accounts, wills, trusts, capital improvements, insurance policies, and beneficiary designations should be up to date and easy to find. You should tell someone you trust where to find these important documents.

## 10 Failing to name your church and other Christian ministries or charities in your estate plan

Have you considered leaving part of your estate to God's work? The government supports your decision to include Christian causes in your estate plan, and such gifts can help reduce your taxes now and later. Tithing (your estate) is not only appropriate, it is a Biblical mandate.

As Brian Kluth reminds us in his book *Because I Love You,* "There are only three places to distribute your estate: family/ friends, ministry/charity, or the government.[3] If you don't do some basic planning, the government may get more than you ever intended, your family may be left confused, angry or shortchanged, and God's work will get nothing."[4]

*"If you wait, all that happens is that you get older."*

*— Larry McMurtry*

# Multiplying a gift

## The legacy of a cafeteria worker

*Linda Flowers was a cafeteria worker in a public school for more than 30 years. She and her late husband had moved into a small house over 50 years ago. After his death in 1972, she continued to live in the house but had neither the funds nor the interest in upkeep or modernization. In 2010 she entered a senior living center and decided to leave her small home to her church where she had been a faithful member for over 30 years. The house at the time of her death was valued at $25,000. It was a very special gift. Then, the men of the church and community all pitched in to modernize and update it. New floors, tile, driveway, paint and other improvements were all added to Linda's legacy. As a result, when her home went on the market, it was valued at over $67,000.*

If a high school cafeteria worker who had little wealth during her lifetime could give such a meaningful gift at her death, what could you do for the sake of the gospel around the world by simply being faithful in your will and estate planning?

Dr. Karl Menninger once asked a very wealthy patient, *"What on earth are you going to do with all that money?"*

The patient replied, a bit reluctantly, *"Just worry about it, I suppose."*

*"Well,"* Menninger went on, *"Do you get that much pleasure out of worrying about it?"*

NOTES

*"No,"* replied the patient, *"but I get such terror when I think of giving it to someone else."*[5]

**A well-prepared will, a carefully chosen executor and a wise estate plan for distributing assets can relieve a lot of worry.** It can also be a blessing to everyone in the family as well as your church, your friends and acquaintances. You cannot hold on to any of your posessions. There are no pockets in a shroud.

# Afterthought

**Creating a will does not have to be a complicated exercise but it is a necessary one. If you do not have a will, you must begin the process immediately. If you have a will, you must be sure that you have reviewed it within the last 3 years.**

A Simple Will needs to be drawn up as soon as possible. You may write your will in your own handwriting. Be sure it is dated and signed. This is the very least you can do today. However, it's better to make a visit to an attorney to draw up a Simple Will that conform to the laws of your state and ensures that your specific wishes can be carried out.

Remember, your state has already written a will for you, and if you die without writing one of your own, your estate may be distributed to relatives other than those you would have specified. Every state has its own rules for who will inherit your property. Usually, only spouses, children and blood relatives will be included under state law. Spouses usually get the largest share.

When there is no will, an unmarried partner, significant other, charities and anyone else you would want to remember will not receive a penny from you. With more couples than ever choosing to live together, plus a continuing high divorce rate, having a will is more important than ever.

Talk to a trusted friend about your personal situation. It may be your spouse, your tax accountant, your banker or the person you choose to be the executor of your estate. Get their advice and guidance. Talk with a recommended attorney. Because of the importance of this document, talk with those you trust and become aware of the laws in your state, either online or by visiting an attorney. But do not delay; little can be gained by waiting and much could be lost.

# Follow-up

You need a will. Use this guide to help you prepare for your conversation with an attorney. Then find an elder law attorney or estate planning attorney either in the yellow pages or by referral. See Chapter 5 for guidance in selecting an attorney.

You have already completed your family information section and your personal property inventory. These are the key elements in creating your will. Now add your list of bequests. Bequests and devices are simply the legal terms for items or property that you leave to someone in your will.

## My personal bequests and devices

The purpose of the will is to honor your requests for the disposition of your property. Your property may include your home and other real estate; tangible personal property such as your cars and furniture; and intangible property like life insurance, bank accounts, stocks, bonds, pension and Social Security benefits.

## Designated beneficiaries

IRA accounts, 401(k)s and other pension plans, bank accounts and insurance policies may have a designated beneficiary named in each document. By signing beneficiary forms you've already determined how those assets will be distributed after death. It's always wise to review beneficiaries as time goes by. A will cannot change the disposition of assets that you have already designated by signing beneficiary forms. **All of your possessions are called your estate.**

# MY WILL

For those who have a current will, complete the follow-up.
For those without a current will, use this as a guide to prepare your
own will and, as soon as possible, take it to your attorney.

| Date written | Where prepared |
|---|---|
| Attorney or other professional help | |
| Contact telephone numbers | |
| Email address | Location of original document |
| Number of copies | Location of copies |
| Executor | Alternate executor |

| SPECIFIC BEQUESTS AND DEVICES |
|---|
| Item, Beneficiary, Alternate Beneficiary |
| |
| |
| |
| |
| |
| |
| |
| |
| |
| |
| |
| |
| |

## SPECIAL DISTRIBUTIONS
*(It is possible to distribute funds from your estate before your estate is settled.)*

### Description, Beneficiary, Alternate Beneficiary

## CHARITIES *(to be remembered by gifts now or memorial gifts)*

### Name, Amount

## REQUESTED MEMORIALS *(in lieu of flowers)*

So watch your step. Use your head. Make the most of every chance you get. These are desperate times! Don't live carelessly, unthinkingly. Make sure you understand what the Master wants.

EPHESIANS 5:15-17

*"Life expectancy would grow by leaps and bounds if green vegetables smelled as good as bacon." — Doug Larson*

We are living in an age of medical miracles: microsurgery, transplants, replacements of hips, knees and other joints, and life support machines and devices for almost every purpose. Medical advances have saved countless lives and enhanced the lifestyles of many who would have been crippled and left immobilized only a few decades ago. But all the advances have also reminded us of the law of unintended consequences. **There is a great difference between living a long life and living a life medically extended.**

## A look ahead

- **Hospitalization statistics you need to know**

- **What is a health care directive?**

- **Who's in charge when you aren't? A Durable Power of Attorney for Health Care**

- **What are the qualifications for a health care advocate?**

- **Palliative care and hospice**

- **Advantages of hospice care**

- **End-of-life discussions**

The odds are there is a hospital in your future. You, a loved one, friend, family member or acquaintance is going to be hospitalized. The advancements in medical care and the advanced specialized care received from hospitals mean that, for a growing number of illnesses, most treatments will be offered only in a hospital. The ease of finding a hospital and the ready availability of hospital care everywhere in the developed world makes the likelihood of hospitalization or outpatient treatment at some point in your life nearly 100%.

# Hospitalization statistics you need to know

Age is a factor in hospitalization. The chance of being admitted to a hospital increases with every birthday. Those 65 years and older are just 13% of the US population but account for 36% of hospital admissions for acute care. One in five people over the age of 65 will have surgery in any given year. Nearly 20% of open-heart procedures are performed on people over 70.

Only 25 years ago, most Americans spent the majority of their final months at home. However, that has quickly changed—not only in America but also in other developed nations. **More than 68% of older adults in the United States pass away in a hospital or nursing home.** Although surveys of healthy adults suggest that a majority would like to die at home, and, despite the rapid growth of the hospice industry in the United States, most Americans still die in hospitals. In 2004, more than 50% of Americans with serious illness died in an acute care hospital and more than 90% of Medicare beneficiaries will be hospitalized in the year prior to their deaths.

NOTES

The last reported statistics in Great Britain indicate that 58% of reported deaths occur in the hospital. In both the United States and Great Britain, this varies from region to region.

According to the Center for Gerontology at Brown University, only 35% of adult deaths in Portland, Oregon, occur in hospitals, compared with 80% in New York City. These differences are partly related to differences in the supply of hospital beds and the availability of alternate care for the dying that is not hospital related.[6]

With this in mind, it is important that you understand and complete a health care directive.

# What is a health care directive?

Never heard of it? Don't be surprised. The New York Times recently reported, "Only about one-third of Americans have completed any kind of advance directive to guide their families and physicians when they cannot speak for themselves. Of the advance directives that have been executed, many, if not most, are too vague to be truly useful."

Research shows the majority of Americans do not understand advance directives. **Of those polled regarding health care, 85% have never heard of a Power of Attorney for Health Care and don't understand the consequences of failing to create one.** Since there is likely to be a hospital in your future, understanding and completing this directive has never been more important. Most states recognize two health care directives: a Living Will and a Durable Power of Attorney for Health Care. To be valid, each one must be signed by two witnesses. It is not necessary to have an attorney prepare these two documents. You may find, however, that discussing them with a disinterested third-party can be very helpful.

## A Living Will

Your right to control the type of medical treatment you receive when you have a terminal condition was clarified in 1990. The United States Supreme Court ruled that if you state your wishes about end-of-life treatment, hospitals, physicians and family members should respect your desires. This is sometimes referred to as the "right to die" and as a Living Will.

A Living Will basically states, "When deciding on treatment, please follow these instructions." It is called a Living Will because it takes effect while you're still alive.[7] In the United States, upon admission to the hospital, you are asked if you have a Living Will. If you do not, you are instructed to complete one while you are there. It's all the more reason to take care of this before admission while you have time to think about it.

**A Living Will details the type of care you want, or don't want, if you have a terminal condition and can no longer express your wishes.** This means you're going to have to make some decisions about your medical treatments if you're unable to speak for yourself. This is much more than a "do not resuscitate" statement.

This is not only a question of which treatment but the duration of the treatment. These are truly end-of-life decisions. Specify the treatment you want and consider how long heroic efforts should continue.

- **If you cannot eat or drink on your own, do you want nutrients and water through a feeding tube or an IV?**
- **If you cannot breathe on your own, do you want to use a respirator to prolong your life?**
- **If your condition is terminal, do you want to continue to receive treatments such as radiation, chemotherapy or dialysis?**
- **Do you want to be kept free of pain and comfortable during a final illness?**

These are not easy questions to answer; be sure to discuss them with your family and physician before any hospitalization.

## *Your written wishes must be made clear*

- What are your feelings on being kept alive artificially?
- What surgical procedures are acceptable in order to keep you alive?

- How does your level of consciousness and ability to communicate affect your quality of life?
- What level of pain management is preferable to you? Do you want to maximize pain relief even if it may interfere with your communication and awareness?

# Do Not Resuscitate order (DNR)

A DNR order sounds ominous. It implies by its very language that life-saving medical procedures will be withheld. But change the language to A Natural Death (AND) and it sounds much different. Yet they both mean the same. Nearly everyone would probably agree that we would all wish a natural death. That order is called AND. It means the same as a DNR. A DNR, or better, AND, is a request to not have cardiopulmonary resuscitation (CPR) if your heart stops or if you stop breathing. (Unless given other instructions, hospital staff will try to revive all patients whose hearts have stopped or who have stopped breathing.) If you do not want to be resuscitated, you must tell your primary physician. **Physicians are the only ones who can write a DNR.** These orders are accepted by doctors and hospitals in all states.

**A DNR is not an order to stop efforts to keep you alive, but it does say that when your heart finally stops that you do not wish to receive CPR or ventilator care.**

Stephen P. Kiernan says, *"A DNR means do all you can to keep me alive, but when I'm dead, then let me go."* [8]

Your Living Will is the basis for all decisions that you or your health care advocate will be making. Be sure you discuss every aspect of your Living Will in detail so your wishes are clearly understood. You can use a DNR order to tell emergency medical personnel that you do not want to receive CPR if there's a medical emergency. Remember that being "kept alive" and "living" may mean two different things. This is one of those heart-wrenching decisions that you can spare your family by having your DNR available whenever you're hospitalized.

## "Five Wishes"

A simple way to create a Living Will is available through **www.agingwithdignity.org.** The document is called "Five Wishes" and is a legal Living Will in 42 states.

### *"Five Wishes" lets your family and doctors know*

- Who you want to make health care decisions for you when you can't make them

- The kind of medical treatment you want or don't want
- How comfortable you want to be
- How you want people to treat you
- What you want your loved ones to know

It is easily downloadable for a small sum or can be sent to you by mail.

# Who's in charge when you aren't? A Durable Power of Attorney for Health Care

In addition to your Living Will, you will need another document: a Durable Power of Attorney for Health Care. This is not the same as a Living Will. This document allows you to designate someone to act on your behalf in regard to your health care when you cannot. This person is sometimes referred to as a proxy, surrogate, representative, agent, advocate or an attorney-in-fact. Sometimes a Durable Power of Attorney for Health Care is referred to as a Health Care Proxy.

**A *Durable* Power of Attorney means that you intend for this document to be effective even if you become disabled or incapacitated.**

Why do you need a Durable Power of Attorney? Because just when you need it most, a simple Power of Attorney ceases to be in effect! At that point, without a Durable Power of Attorney, you will need to go through the expense and embarrassment of having a court-appointed guardian.

NOTES

Remember, your agent gains enormous power over your medical care when you can no longer communicate your wishes to your doctors and hospital staff.

Your medical advocate expresses how you want to be treated. For example, he or she can decide

- which hospital treats you
- what doctor or doctors are your attending physicians
- whether or not you will have a particular surgery
- what particular drugs you will or will not take

A Durable Power of Attorney for Health Care gives your agent the power to make every decision regarding your health care other than the decisions regarding termination of life support.

## A health care advocate

The designation of a health care advocate is contained in a Living Will Directive or your Durable Power of Attorney for Health Care. A Living Will Directive doesn't go into effect unless you no longer have "decisional capacity." This means a health care surrogate designation does not take effect until the attending physician and one other physician certify that you are "permanently unconscious" or have a "terminal" condition. **This does not mean withholding treatment or any act to shorten life. It simply means permitting the natural process of dying.**

When it comes to picking the right person to serve as your health care advocate, take your time, think it through and get it right. You're giving this person the ability to act if you're no longer able to act for yourself. You are putting your life in his or her hands. Here again the question is, "Whom do you trust?"

Think carefully—my integrity is on the line! Can you detect anything false in what I say? Don't you trust me to discern good from evil?

JOB 6:29

# What are the qualifications for a health care advocate?

Here are some things to consider when deciding whom to choose for this important role:

## Questions for you to answer

- Will this person be with me in the hospital?
- Does this person really know what I want?

- Will this person respect my wishes?
- How well do I know this person and is he or she respected by my family?
- How will this person respond if family members disagree with my wishes?
- Is this person emotionally capable of making life-and-death decisions?
- Does this person benefit financially at my death?

The right person for you will be the person you believe is best able to act on your behalf. It may be your spouse, a close friend or one of your children. You should always select an alternate agent. It may not be possible for your first choice to serve for a number of reasons. But do not choose two or more to serve together. A dispute would defeat the whole point of having a health care advocate. States place restrictions on who may be selected. Health care providers are usually prohibited unless that person is also your spouse or a close relative. The person must be an adult.

You can get more free information on health care directives from your doctor or by visiting any hospital or nursing home. The Internet will provide a lot of guidance and state-specific forms. Your state requirements can be found at **www.caringinfo.org**. This is the website of the National Hospice and Palliative Care Organization.

**You must have your health care directive easily accessible and close by at all times. Do not put it in a safe deposit box or file it where you can't find it. You may be going to the hospital on a moment's notice. Put it where you and your family can find it. Give copies to your health care advocate, your medical team and others who ought to know your wishes.**

NOTES

# Palliative care and hospice

Here are two more terms that many are not very familiar with but are very important when it comes to understanding and dealing with end-of-life issues. Evidence suggests that palliative care and hospice add to the quality as well as the quantity of your life.

## Palliative care

Palliative care is the medical specialty focused on relief of the pain, stress and other debilitating symptoms of serious illness. The goal is to relieve suffering and provide the best possible quality of life for patients and their families.

Palliative care relieves symptoms such as pain, shortness of breath, fatigue, nausea, loss of appetite and difficulty sleeping. It helps patients gain the strength for daily life; it improves their ability to tolerate medical treatments and helps them better understand their choices for care. Overall, palliative care offers patients and their families the best possible quality of life during their illness. In fact, the American Medical Association (AMA) released a study confirming that palliative care makes an enormous difference in cancer patients' quality of life.

*Palliative care may begin at the time of diagnosis or any time during treatment. It is concerned with the emotional, spiritual, and practical needs of the patient and those close to them. Palliative care is important for those who are thought to be at imminent risk of dying, those who are extremely ill, or those who are living with serious complications in the final stages of chronic diseases.[9]*

There are a number of hospitals that specialize in palliative care. Many hospitals have a team of experts including doctors, nurses and social workers. Chaplains, massage therapists, pharmacists, nutritionists and others might also be part of the team. *(When my brother was hospitalized with terminal lung cancer, a palliative care team was there to help in any way possible. A grilled cheese sandwich and tomato soup at midnight was not too much to ask.)*

## Hospice care

**Hospice Inc. was established in the United States in 1971 although its origins can be traced back much earlier in history.**

Hospice is a concept rooted in the centuries-old idea of offering a place of shelter and rest, or "hospitality," to weary and sick travelers on a long journey. In 1967, Dame

Cicely Saunders at St. Christopher's Hospice in London first applied the term "hospice" to specialized care for dying patients. Today, hospice care provides humane and compassionate care for people in the last phases of incurable disease so that they may live the remainder of their lives as comfortably as possible.

The hospice philosophy accepts death as the final stage of life. **The goal of hospice is to enable patients to continue an alert, pain-free life and to manage other symptoms so that their last days may be spent with dignity and quality, surrounded by their loved ones.** Hospice affirms life and does not hasten or postpone death. Hospice care can be given in the patient's home, a hospital, nursing home or private hospice facility. Hospice care treats the symptoms but does not cure the disease; its main purpose is to improve your quality of life.[10]

And just to make it confusing, the word "hospice" also refers to a facility that provides hospice care, such as a specialized center. The hospice (place) can be located within a separate building or can be housed within a hospital or nursing home. Hospice (care) can also be provided at home. It may include case management by a hospice nurse, access to a hospice physician and drugs at no cost if they are related to the terminal diagnosis and

*"You matter because of who you are. You matter to the last moment of your life, and we will do all we can, not only to help you die peacefully, but also to live until you die."*

— *Dame Cicely Saunders*

are palliative as determined by the hospice plan of care.

Hospice, both the place and the care (in-home care, inpatient care, continuous care, and respite care) can be paid for by your insurance plan. Home hospice care usually costs less than care in hospitals, nursing homes, or other institutional settings; less high-cost technology is used and family and friends provide most of the care at home.

Medicare, Medicaid in some states, the Department of Veterans Affairs, most private insurance plans, HMOs, and other managed care organizations pay for hospice care. Community contributions, memorial donations, and foundation gifts allow many hospices to give free services to patients who can't afford payment. Some programs charge patients according to their ability to pay.

**Access to hospice care is based on two conditions:**

1 A physician must certify that he or she believes the patient has a life expectancy of 6 months or less if the disease runs its expected course.

2 The patient (or proxy) must elect hospice care. In doing so, he or she agrees that the care will be managed by the hospice program.

**A person may withdraw from hospice at any time.** If a patient is referred to hospice (both care and place), his or her doctor must also decide whether to remain the physician of record or to refer the patient to the hospice medical director.

# Advantages of hospice care

Unlike a hospital where the requirements for regular testing, blood work, taking blood pressure, taking the pulse, temperature reading and a wide variety of interruptions can go on both day and night, hospice tries to provide quiet and privacy for both the patient and the family. This may make these final days much more comfortable and meaningful than hospital care. In fact, some evidence suggests that life is actually prolonged while in a hospice facility. Less stress may mean a longer life. The patient's quality of life may also be improved during this period of terminal care.

**Remember, hospice does not continue treatment for the disease of a terminal patient. Hospice care treats the symptoms of a disease. Hospice is a positive and compassionate choice when the finality of life and the awareness of approaching the end of life is apparent to the patient and family.**

# End-of-life discussions

It seems that, in spite of the growing need to talk about the end of life, everyone avoids the topic.

Survey after survey indicates that most patients want to have these discussions. The same surveys note that they are not occurring. For example, a 2005 AARP survey in Massachusetts of members over age 50 found that 89% of those polled rated having honest answers from their doctor about terminal conditions as very important, but only 17% had discussed their preferences for such care with their physicians. **Let me repeat: 89% of those surveyed wanted to have end-of-life discussions, but only 17% discussed their preferences with their physicians.**

Here is a blog post by a gentleman from Georgia that provides insight into why some choose not to have these discussions:

*I am a senior, 65 years old. I have never discussed end-of-life issues with my doctor. I thought about it when my mom died, and when my dad died, but never felt so strongly that I brought it up to my doctor. I have enough trouble trying to remember everything I need to talk to him about staying alive. I always make a list of things to ask but most of the time I don't get to ask all of them.*

*If he brought up the subject, I don't know exactly how I would feel about it. I guess I would immediately wonder if something showed up in my blood work that made him mention it. I know I should have an advance directive, but procrastination seems to be holding more sway with me right now. Maybe when I get old....* [11]

Putting it off, even when reminded of its importance, is all too common. Plus, this blogger says if the doctor brings it up, it would be a cause for worry. Yet study after study also shows that patients continue to die in pain, on ventilators, and in the intensive care unit, though many of them did not want such treatment at the end of their lives.

- The Robert Wood Johnson study "Means to a Better End: A Report on Dying in America Today" found that 42% of all nursing home residents were persistently in pain.
- The Dartmouth Atlas of Health Care found that, although the majority of Americans say they would prefer to die at home, 50% of deaths take place in a hospital and 18% of those are in the intensive care unit.[12]

In another study funded by the Robert Wood Johnson Foundation at the University of Washington at Seattle, researchers scored the impact of dying at home versus the hospital or other medical settings. Families' scores were significantly more positive for the deceased who
- died at home
- died in their preferred setting
- discussed their end-of-life care preferences with a loved one
- received care in line with their preferences
- felt listened to by their health care team

**When physicians are asked why they do not regularly engage in advance-care planning with their patients, they reply that they do not have the time for such conversations.**

Recent legislation was under consideration in Congress that would allow physicians to be reimbursed for an advance-care planning discussion with their patients. But the "death panel" interpretation of this needed discussion entirely missed the point and the legislation failed to get the support it needed. Before Congress adjourned in 2010, a bill was passed permitting physicians to take the time and be paid for end-of-life discussion, but was then dropped from the legislation.

Not only do doctors have limited time but hospital stays are being shortened. During the period 1980-2000, the average length of an inpatient hospital stay fell from 7.5 days to 4.9 days. The result is less time to talk and a higher overall concentration of sick people who need more care.[13]

**Being admitted to the hospital will never be on anyone's list of "must do's." But when it's a necessary be sure to take copies of your health care directives as well as your hospital insurance cards, a list of any allergies you may have and your current medications .**

Charlie Viraola had this unusual idea when it comes to staying out of the hospital: "I had my appendix removed. There was nothing wrong with it, I did it just as a warning to the other organs in my body to shape up or they are out of there."

What if the roof falls in, and your whole life goes to pieces?
What if catastrophe strikes and there is nothing to show for your life but rubble and ashes?

PROVERBS 1:27

# Afterthought

It seems many think of going to the hospital as a last resort. A number of people say they don't want to go to the hospital even when their symptoms indicate a serious illness. Often it's because of the lack of health insurance or a fear of doctors or medical procedures. An unspoken reason is many people believe the hospital is where you go to die. However, many find that it is also a place where you find healing and hope.

If you prepare the proper documents before you go to the hospital, discuss your thoughts, concerns and wishes before you are admitted, it will ease fears and make hospitalization and treatment a much easier decision for you and your family.

Advanced health care directives are little known by the general public. Put your new knowledge to work. Get the "Five Wishes" booklet mentioned earlier or download the forms from the **www.ForeTalkSeminar.com** website. Or better yet, when you write your will, have your attorney draw up your Living Will and your Durable Power of Attorney for Health Care.

Federal regulations now require that everyone admitted to a hospital must be informed about the necessity of a Living Will. In case of a serious illness that could be life threatening the hospital is going to ask you to complete a Living Will. There is no law requiring a Durable Power of Attorney for Health Care, yet with all the ways a patient can become incapacitated, unable to make decisions for themselves, this document is a necessity. An attorney is not required for preparing a Living Will or a Do Not Resuscitate order. Every state has its own laws and, while they are similar, they are not the same. A helpful website with updated information to review state law across the country is www.findlaw.com.

A Durable Power of Attorney for Health Care ought to be prepared by an attorney. This gives you the opportunity to discuss this serious document and its implications with a third party who knows your state laws and how they are currently being applied.

Earlier in *ForeTalk*, we discussed the situations we need to address before the end of our lives. Hospitalization or potential hospitalization is one of those situations. Now is the ideal time to take care of the legal documents needed—a will, a Durable Power of Attorney for Finances (see p. 68), a Durable Power of Attorney for Health Care and a Living Will. Write your last letter and prepare thoughtfully for what you know lies ahead. These are truly life and death documents and, even though legal guidance may not be required, it may be the intelligent decision.

Turn to the appendix or download the information from the *ForeTalk* website, www.ForeTalkSeminar.com. Read over the documents and discuss the implications and possible conclusions with those you trust. Right now, on your *ForeTalk* planning guide, give yourself a checkmark for understanding and planning advanced health care directives.

# PRAYER

*Dear Heavenly Father, there are times in our lives when our bodies are in pain without relief. The pain tells us that something is wrong and that it needs attention. When it is a physical pain, Lord, help us to be mindful of our stewardship of the body You have given us and to take good care of it. When it is mental anguish, guide us to seek comfort and wise counsel. Help us to see the value of the medical profession and appreciate those who have spent long years of study to provide us their insight and skill as well as practice Your own gifts of healing. Make us aware when we need the services of health care professionals. Give us the wisdom to plan ahead for those times, and grant us confidence not only in those who minister to us in medical care but also in the living power of our Savior Who was Himself called, "the Great Physician."* AMEN

# Follow-up

## YOUR CHECKLIST
*A health care directive includes two documents.*
*Put a check by the ones you've completed and the date completed.*

| | |
|---|---|
| ☐ A Living Will | Date |
| ☐ A Durable Power of Attorney for Health Care | Date |

These two documents should be kept together so that they can be taken with you when you are admitted to the hospital or experiencing any medical emergency.

Where have you filed these documents?

Whom have you chosen to serve as your health care surrogate or attorney-in-fact?
(You may choose the same person for both.)

Give yourself a checkmark when:

☐ You have discussed your choice of a health care surrogate or attorney-in-fact with the person you've selected as well as others who should know, including your physician.

☐ You have chosen an alternative health-care surrogate or attorney-in-fact.
*Name:*

☐ You have visited or received information about hospice care in your community.

☐ You have discussed with your spouse, significant other or the most important people in your life, your beliefs about a Do Not Resuscitate order.

Some personal questions for you to consider. These questions are entirely for your benefit. Answer them honestly. Your answers will tell you a lot about yourself and how well you are taking care of your own health. Cancer, heart conditions, strokes and other often fatal diseases, when detected in the early stages of development, can frequently be cured before they become life threatening.

Do you have regularly scheduled physicals?

When was your last comprenhensive physical?

| What medications are you taking currently and what condition do they treat? | | |
|---|---|---|
| MEDICATION | DOSAGE | CONDITION |
| 1 | | |
| 2 | | |
| 3 | | |
| 4 | | |
| 5 | | |
| 6 | | |
| 7 | | |
| 8 | | |

What supplements are you taking?

Who is your family physician?

Telephone number

| What specialists have you seen? | |
|---|---|
| **NAMES and TELEPHONE NUMBERS** | |

| | |
|---|---|
| 1 | |
| 2 | |
| 3 | |
| 4 | |
| 5 | |
| 6 | |
| 7 | |
| 8 | |
| 9 | |

What personal habits may be putting your life at risk?

A steady smoker takes 15 years off of his or her life on the average. My brother would have given every cent he paid for cigarettes over his lifetime just for another year of life. Don't ignore the facts. Smoking, alcohol abuse or drug abuse, poor diet and lack of exercise are all threats to our well-being, but are actions over which we have some control. Give yourself a checkmark if you recognize and are willing to change habits that are destructive to your well-being.

☐ I am making a personal decision to take charge of my life by changing destructive behaviors that harm me and, indirectly, those I love.

| SIGNED | DATE |
|---|---|
| | |

Tell those rich in this world's wealth to quit being so full of themselves and so obsessed with money, which is here today and gone tomorrow. Tell them to go after God, who piles on all the riches we could ever manage.   I TIMOTHY 6:17

*These words appeared in the church bulletin:*
*"The Lord loves the cheerful giver.*
*He also accepts from a grouch."*

Our financial vocabulary has expanded over the last several years to include a number of new words and expressions. Many of these terms were unfamiliar to us just a decade or so ago. Euros, money market funds, Exchange Traded Funds (or ETFs), flexible spending accounts, cash cards and online banking are just a few of the new terms in the daily news.

When it comes to understanding finances, not everyone is on the same page. It is still possible to graduate from high school and college without taking one class in basic economics. As a result, there is a financial illiteracy across every demographic in America. When you combine these new terms with a financial illiteracy and our increasing longevity, a potential problem becomes apparent.

**What if an age-related or medical problem resulted in your being incapacitated for a time? Who would handle all the details of managing your daily affairs, paying bills, depositing checks, arranging and paying for medical care, and taking care of your family?** Who would you give power over your financial affairs and what power would you give them? That's what this chapter is about.

*Get wisdom—it's worth more than money; choose insight over income every time.* PROVERBS 16:16

## A look ahead

- **What is a Durable Power of Attorney for Finances?**
- **What should you look for when selecting your agent?**
- **How much power in a Durable Power of Attorney for Finances?**
- **When does a Durable Power of Attorney for Finances take effect?**
- **Reviewing and revoking powers of attorney**
- **The dangers of joint ownership and incapacity**

Money has often been a taboo subject in many households. Husbands and wives don't discuss their finances. Children are seldom informed about money matters within the family. On the job, employees don't discuss salaries with each other and, in fact, usually only discuss money with their bosses once a year at their salary review. Entrepreneurs and the self-employed look at money differently from those who have earned every dollar working for someone else, but they still don't discuss money matters.

**Most of us would agree with the comedian Jackie Mason who said he had enough money to last, as long as he didn't spend any.**

# What is a Durable Power of Attorney for Finances?

No matter what your view of money, it is one of the key end-of-life issues. We have already discussed the importance of having a will—which only comes into force at your death. But what about while you are alive? Whom would you trust to manage your financial affairs? Wait just a second. If I'm alive, why would I want someone else to manage my affairs? That question is more relevant than ever before. Accidents, illness or the effects of aging can be incapacitating.

Your will designates your wishes after your death in regard to your assets. **But you also need another document, a Durable Power of Attorney for Finances. This document provides for someone to act on your behalf in money matters in case you are incapacitated.**

Managing money is not easy. It takes hard work to make money, discipline to save it, skill to make it grow, and insight to manage it well. The question in this chapter is not "Can you do it well?" Rather, the question is "Who do you believe can do it well on your behalf?"

Periods of incapacity may be brief as result of an accident or illness, or they may linger for long periods of time. **Unless you create a Durable Power of Attorney for Finances, there will be difficulty in managing your financial affairs if you are incapacitated.**

Remember, a Power of Attorney is a document in which you grant certain authority to another person to act on your behalf. **In most states, a Power of Attorney is not valid if you become incapacitated unless it's a Durable Power of Attorney.**

## A Durable Power of Attorney for Finances

- Clearly states that you intend the power of attorney to continue to be valid if you become disabled or incapacitated
- Remains in effect until you revoke it or you pass away

68

- Grants legal authority to your agent or your proxy to manage your financial affairs
- Defines the powers of your agent and any limits you want to place on his or her authority

A Durable Power of Attorney will be there when you need it most—if you are incapacitated. Choosing the one who will act as your Power of Attorney for Finances is a question of major significance.

# What should you look for when selecting your agent?

*"They, who are of the opinion that Money will do everything, may very well be suspected to do everything for Money."*
*– George Savile*

The person you choose will have a great deal of control over your assets and most often will serve without any oversight. **You should select someone in whom you have absolute confidence.**

## Questions you must answer

- Do you trust this person with a blank check?

- Is he or she willing to serve in this difficult position?
- Does he or she have the time to give to this responsibility?
- Are you comfortable talking about your financial affairs with this individual?
- Does this person have personal financial stability?
- Does he or she have any financial interests that may conflict with yours or others in your family?

If you are married, the wisest decision may be to choose your spouse as your agent. In addition to the emotional ones, there are both legal and practical reasons why this makes sense. Choosing someone other than your spouse opens the door for conflict over managing assets that belong to both spouses; however, if you don't have a spouse or if for any reason your spouse is not equipped to manage your financial affairs, naming someone else may be your only choice. **No matter whom you choose, it should be carefully discussed with your family. Remember, money is a sensitive subject, especially when someone is acting on your behalf.**

Because a Durable Power of Attorney for Finances can give broad power to the person you select, you have a wide range of choices in the powers you grant.

However, legally, he or she may not
- make, amend or revoke your will
- enact a health care proxy on your behalf
- use the assets of your estate for personal benefit unless you've authorized such use

You can also authorize your agent to be paid for the service. If you do not specifically provide for payment, the agent may not be compensated for any service he or she performs. If you grant compensation, specify the amount. If you don't, he or she can claim reasonable fees, which can mean many things to many people. In some cases the court may determine what fee is reasonable. Protect yourself and your agent by stating an amount for compensation.

# How much power in a Durable Power of Attorney for Finances?

Our lives have become much more complicated in recent years. Divorce and remarriage; changing jobs; moving from one state to another or owning property in two or more states; having multiple bank accounts with several financial institutions; having more than one retirement plan, pension or savings account—all call for a carefully written Durable Power of Attorney for Finances.

You decide what powers you grant to your agent. Most often, he or she is granted power to manage your expenses and pay your bills. That means writing checks on your account. Bank accounts and banking transactions are often taken care of by the authority you grant in this document.

## Powers you may grant to your agent

- Access your safe deposit box
- Collect, cash or deposit government benefits
- Invest your money
- Make gifts to individuals as well as institutions
- Purchase insurance and annuities
- Pay taxes
- Make legal claims on your behalf
- Buy, rent and sell real estate
- Improve and manage your real estate
- Run your business
- Amend trust agreements
- Hire or fire attorneys, nurses, caretakers
- Use your assets such as your automobile

Be very careful when choosing your agent. If you have any question about your choice, discuss it with an attorney. Do not risk your future on a person who may not be worthy of your trust or capable of managing your affairs. Serving as an agent for a Durable Power of Attorney for Finances is a heavy responsibility. It is also a position in which complete confidence is required. It's wise to have an alternate agent just in case your first choice becomes unwilling, unable to serve or, for some reason, must be replaced. If you do not designate a replacement, and your first choice is unable to fulfill the responsibilities, your Power of Attorney will fail.

In some cases, your agent may appoint his or her own successor.

> *"I trust everybody;*
> *it's just the devil in them*
> *that I don't trust."*
>
> *– Donald Sutherland in*
> *"The Italian Job"*

A Durable Power of Attorney for Finances is no simple matter. Attorneys can tell tragic stories about theft from estates, financial incompetence, and total mismanagement resulting from selecting the wrong person as an agent.

# When does a Durable Power of Attorney for Finances take effect?

You can state when you want the Durable Power of Attorney to go into effect. You can have it take effect immediately or, if you wish, when you can no longer manage your financial affairs. If you want to give your agent permission to start handling your finances right away, you can still maintain control by explaining what you want done and your agent is legally obligated to follow your directions. **If you ever become dis-satisfied, you can revoke the Durable**

**Power of Attorney and the authority granted.**

You can also decide that your Durable Power of Attorney will only become effective if you become incapacitated. This is called a Springing Power of Attorney. It won't take effect unless a physician examines you and declares, in writing, that you cannot manage your finances. This can be legally complicated. Some states do not recognize a Springing Power of Attorney. If you trust your agent and selected him or her carefully, you may find it makes more sense just to create a document that becomes effective immediately and then make it clear to your agent when to act on your behalf in financial matters.

# Reviewing and revoking powers of attorney

Not every decision we make is always the right one. Time changes things. People change. Therefore, it's very important to review your Durable Powers of Attorney to make sure that they continue to reflect your wishes. You also want to verify your choice of agents as well as any successors you may have identified.

Whenever there is a major change in your life such as marriage, a new child, grandchild, divorce, retirement, or any kind of relocation or financial change, take the time to review all of your estate documents to be sure that they are current. It is not uncommon to have a document written years ago appointing executors and agents and naming beneficiaries and co-beneficiaries who are now deceased. **It is wise to review all of your estate documents every 3 years or so.**

When you want to revoke your Power of Attorney, you provide written notice to your agent, anyone who has a copy of the document as well as any bank or financial institution where your agent may have already used your Power of Attorney. Some states require a formal notice of revocation with the recorder of deeds in the city or county where you live and in any county or country where you own real estate.

# A Non-durable Power of Attorney

A periodic power of attorney, or renewable power of attorney, is one that is enacted with a predetermined termination date. There may be times it would be wise to use this Non-durable Power of Attorney. Usually this type of document is used when you plan to be away, take a long vacation, leave the country or are hospitalized. A Non-durable Power of Attorney will end at your incapacity or death. Because this is a temporary document, most adults still need to prepare a permanent document.

**This question arises with every legal document: "Should I have an attorney draw up these documents?" In most circumstances the answer is the same: "Yes."**

These are significant and important documents that address your personal well-being. While doing it yourself is always an option and fill-in-the blank forms are available online, no form matches the specific needs of every individual. The best idea may be to use these forms to provide your attorney with your pertinent information and have him or her prepare your will. In doing this, you may reduce the time involved and the attorney fees.

# The dangers of joint ownership and incapacity

Joint Ownership, or Joint Tenancy with the Right of Survivorship (JTWROS), is a common form of property ownership. Right of survivorship means that when one joint owner dies, the surviving owner or owners own 100% of the property. It's a convenient way to allow another person access to your assets or to deposit or write checks on your behalf.

**The mistake that many people make is thinking that joint ownership is a substitute for other planning tools.** It is not. In fact, joint ownership has a serious disadvantage when one of the partners is incapacitated. Transfers of a car or securities

normally require the signature of both owners. The loss of capacity of one owner can prevent a needed sale or transfer of property. Here is just one example:

*Alton and Anna had been married for over 40 years. All of their accounts were joint tenancy. Alton had developed Alzheimer's disease, which was slowly incapacitating him, and he needed care that Anna could not provide at home. How would they pay for it? Where would they live? Would they be together? Anna decided they would sell the house and withdraw the assets in his 401(k) account. However, because Alton was incapacitated, he couldn't sign any of the documents required for the sale of the house or withdraw funds from his 401(k). Without a Durable Power of Attorney for Finances, Anna had no way to find the money to provide for his care and new living arrangements. It took a court order and the attorney over a year to solve a problem that could have been taken care of by having foretalk with a trusted advisor.*

*"Do your givin'
while you're livin'
and then your knowin'
where it's goin'."*

*– Anonymous*

# Afterthought

A Durable Power of Attorney for Finances is a powerful document and a necessity for everyone who owns property in joint names or has assets in his or her individual name. Incapacity, like an accident, cannot be predicted but we must prepare for the possibility. The law requires that people must have capacity to create a Durable Power of Attorney. A physician or other mental health specialist may be required to examine and determine that the standards of capacity are met. Without capacity none of these documents can be created. The time is now. In states that allow property to be held as community property or as marital property, there may be additional complications. An attorney is your best source of guidance.

Having a will is not an estate plan. Having an estate plan means having all the documents necessary to settle your affairs. That includes a Durable Power of Attorney for Finances. It will authorize your agent to act for you with respect to money and property if you are in the hospital for a few weeks, out of the country for a few months or incapacitated over a long period of time. Without a Durable Power of Attorney for Finances, those whom you love most can run into a buzz saw of family conflicts and legal complications.

A Durable Power of Attorney for Finances is not only desirable to protect you and your family, it also authorizes financial institutions to work with the individual you've selected to act on your behalf. If you don't take the time to create one now while you are competent, the only alternative for your family will be to have the court name someone. That will be expensive. It is also restrictive and public. Taking care of your finances may mean more than writing checks. There may be property to be sold—securities, houses, boats and cars. You may need someone to find and pay for an assisted living center or nursing home. To do any of these things, you need to give the authority that a Durable Power of Attorney for Finances provides.

Now that you understand the significance of a Durable Power of Attorney for Finances, make this critical conversation happen now. Come to an agreement with your family concerning who your agent should be and then discuss decisions important to you if you are ever incapacitated. Talk with your agent about the importance of this document.

A will is not enough; joint tenancy (JTWROS) is not complete enough. Your estate plan needs a Durable Power of Attorney for Finances. Selecting the right person to guide your financial future and help your loved ones with financial decisions is a clear recognition of your care and compassion for your family.

# PRAYER

*Our Dear Heavenly Father,* we are so grateful for family, for the loving people in our lives, for all the blessings that make this life a wonderful adventure. It is my prayer that the future may reflect every aspect of my love for You and for those You have given me to love. Grant me the wisdom to make the right choices, the kind of choices that will clearly demonstrate not only my love and affection for the most meaningful people in my life, but also my awareness of Your amazing grace. Thank You for all that has been a part of our lives and for the future that lies ahead, made even more promising by the attention given to making that financial future more secure through these choices made today.  AMEN

# Follow-up

**If you are incapacitated or at your death, your Durable Power of Attorney for Finances names the person who can manage your financial affairs on your behalf.**

| Who is your first choice to serve as your agent? | |
| --- | --- |
| Name | Email |
| Address | |
| Cell phone | Home phone |
| Successor or alternate | |
| Name | Email |
| Address | |
| Cell phone | Home phone |
| What financial powers do you want to grant to your agent? | |
| ☐ Y ☐ N  Sell, mortgage, exchange, lease or manage real estate | |
| ☐ Y ☐ N  Buy, sell, exchange, or manage personal property | |

| | |
|---|---|
| ☐ Y ☐ N | Control bank and financial interests |
| ☐ Y ☐ N | Control any insurance or annuity policy |
| ☐ Y ☐ N | Act for me in estate, trust, and other beneficiary transactions |
| ☐ Y ☐ N | Act for me by managing assets transferred to any living trust I may have |
| ☐ Y ☐ N | Act for me in all claims and litigation matters |
| ☐ Y ☐ N | Act for me in securing all governmental benefits owed to me |
| ☐ Y ☐ N | Act for me in all matters regarding my retirement plans and benefits |
| ☐ Y ☐ N | Continue to provide for the well-being, education, medical care for me and my family |
| ☐ Y ☐ N | Take any action to meet tax obligations |
| ☐ Y ☐ N | Provide gifts to family on special occasions |
| ☐ Y ☐ N | Continue providing gifts to charities as I have in the past |
| ☐ Y ☐ N | Employ or dismiss any professionals for my care and the care of my family |

Are there additional powers you wish to grant?

|  |
|---|
|  |
|  |
|  |

The two witnesses to my Durable Power of Attorney for Finances are:

| Name | Phone |
|---|---|
| Name | Phone |

## YOUR CHECKLIST

| | |
|---|---|
| ☐ I have discussed my wishes with my agent | Date |
| ☐ My documents are prepared and signed | Date |

☐ I have shared with others where the documents are located

☐ My Durable Power of Attorney for Finances has been delivered to my financial institutions.

☐ I have requested copies of transactions in my account be sent to my attorney as well as the successor agent for my Durable Power of Attorney for Finances.

Without good direction, people lose their way; the more wise counsel you follow, the better your chances.

PROVERBS 11:14

*You have the right to remain silent. Anything you say will be misquoted, and then used against you.* – *Anonymous*

A good lawyer is a friend indeed and will become your trusted advisor. Finding the right attorney to get quality advice and guidance is a critical step your family will long appreciate.

## A look ahead

- **Who needs to hire an attorney and why?**
- **When is an attorney not needed?**
- **How to find the right attorney**
- **Elder law**
- **Creating your estate plan**
- **The estate tax tango**

# Who needs to hire an attorney and why?

Occasionally the news will tell the story of a defendant who decided to defend himself before the court. Why would anyone do that and risk years of imprisonment or even death? Why would you not want to be represented by an attorney? **Although in our country we may represent ourselves and create documents recognized by the courts, in my opinion it is seldom a correct decision.** Consulting an attorney about any legal problem is usually a smart thing to do. Even if you choose not to have the attorney represent you, discussing your concerns with an experienced and wise advisor ought to be your starting place in any legal matter. In the world we live in, the changes in family structure, health care, taxation and estate planning have moved dying away from being a quiet personal matter to being a public and legal affair. Working with a good attorney to protect and preserve your family values as well as valuable assets accumulated over a lifetime can provide a high level of confidence for every member of the family.

**Typically, we consult an attorney only when we have a legal problem. However, when it comes to end-of-life matters, consulting an attorney is done to *prevent* legal problems.**

Who needs to consult an attorney? Everyone whose marital status, business relationships, family conflicts, property ownership or anything that may cause confusion and/or conflict needs an attorney.

# When is an attorney not needed?

There are a number of online legal guides and document websites. There are also a number of books available that recommend an individual create his or her own simple will. One author suggests, "The law is on your side—it wants to make it easy for people to make their last wishes binding. Your best bet is to use a do-it-yourself online tool or software that will guide you through the decision-making process and provide the legal language that will make it easy for your heirs to settle your estate." [14]

> *The 50-50-90 rule:*
> *"Anytime you have*
> *a 50-50 chance of getting*
> *something right, there is*
> *a 90% probability that*
> *you'll get it wrong."*
>
> *– Andy Rooney*

**Have you ever visited a home supply warehouse?** It is filled with do-it-yourself handymen and women. Some look as if they could tear down a house and rebuild it from the ground up while others couldn't tell a crescent wrench from a crescent roll. That's not a problem unless you get confused about which one best describes your skills. Having a set of blueprints doesn't mean you can build a house that others will live in.

Remember, when it comes to end-of-life planning, the reason for consulting an attorney is to prevent problems later for your heirs. However, there are times the do-it-yourself option, though not recommended, may work.

### 1 When there are no assets

There are individuals and families who either chose not to accumulate assets or who were unable to accumulate assets. Without assets, there is no need for a will. Few are in this category.

### 2 When there are limited assets

Those who have limited assets simply mean those without real estate, investment accounts, 401(k)s or annuities. A simple will often suffices to pass along automobiles, collectibles, jewelry or other personal items. Some authorities believe that if your assets are less than $100,000 and you have no special-needs minor children, you may not need to consult an attorney.

### 3 When there is confidence in the knowledge, skill and ability to understand and implement legal requirements

There are numerous places to find information and fill-in-the-blank forms. If your experience, education or interest has prepared you to complete this task with confidence that this document can be defended in court, then you may not need an attorney.

### 4 When there are simple legal relationships

When there is no spouse or only one spouse and/or children from a single marriage, it may not be necessary to consult an attorney. The simpler your life, the easier it is to do without the services of an attorney. This is especially true when your assets are limited and your relationships have always been stable. Even then, a legal review would be helpful.

Everyone else should consult an attorney. I have found that even in the simplest matters, such as traffic court, an attorney can make all the difference in whether or not a traffic ticket results in a license suspension, points subtracted or paying a fine for a lesser charge. **Our lack of knowledge about the law and its provisions has an impact on every legal matter.** A good attorney will be one of your most trusted resources and advisors.

# How to find the right attorney

## 1 Referrals
One of the very best ways to find an attorney is to ask your friends, business acquaintances, pastor or church leaders for recommendations. But be sure to tell them what kind of attorney you want. Not every attorney is skilled and qualified in dealing with matters of elder law, wills and trusts. Remember what you've always heard about someone who is a "jack of all trades."

## 2 Interviews
Once you have made a list of attorneys, call each one, tell him or her of your interest and ask for an appointment. This is how attorneys find new clients, and most are willing to give you some of their time at no cost to see if their services will be appropriate for you. Speak to several attorneys before you make your decision. You want to find an attorney who not only has good legal skills but excellent interpersonal skills as well. You and your family may be spending many hours with the person you choose, so take the time to find the right match.

Lloyd Price hit the charts in 1959 with a great song and solid advice—"Personality." It contained a lot of wisdom.

NOTES

When you are looking to build a relationship, personality cannot be overlooked. It doesn't matter who referred the attorney; your choice must be someone you feel comfortable with during your visit. How you are treated will tell you a lot about that person's style and whether or not it fits you.

## 3 What to ask

Write down the questions you want to ask before you go to the interview.

- What is his or her experience in wills and trusts?
- How much of his or her practice is in this area of the law?
- What is the best way to contact him or her? Phone or email? How often is appropriate?
- How long will it take to have your calls returned?
- How much time should it take to complete your estate plan?
- How will you be billed?

Almost nothing is more aggravating than leaving a legal project in a lawyer's hands and then have weeks or even months go by without knowing what is happening. You want a lawyer who will work hard on your behalf and follow through promptly.

Ideally, you would like an estimate on cost. You will find that attorneys are happy to provide this. Most attorneys will bill by the hour although some have set fees for different projects or tasks. A good attorney will bill you only for time in conversation with you or actually devoted to your case.

Everyone benefits when both parties understand billing and fees. Being a good client is just as important as finding a good attorney. Expect to pay for all the work that has been done on your behalf. Pay on time and consider the expense you are saving your heirs by doing this correctly now.

# Elder law

Attorneys, like doctors, have specialties. There are criminal lawyers, corporate lawyers, trial lawyers, personal injury lawyers, domestic relations lawyers, tax attorneys and many other specialties. Our laws cover virtually every aspect of life and specialized attorneys are available to provide guidance and assistance. It should be no surprise that the rapid growth of older Americans in the United States and around the world has led to a new law specialty: elder law. This may be one of the most valuable and yet largely unknown specialties in the United States.

**The National Academy of Elder Law Attorneys, Inc. (NAELA) was founded in 1987 as a professional association of attorneys who are dedicated to improving the quality of legal services provided to seniors and people with special needs.**

The attorneys who are members of this national academy are those who have a specific interest in elder law. They have advanced training in preparing documents relating to wills and trusts, estate planning, powers of attorney, medicare and medicaid law and other topics of interest to older Americans. Elder law attorneys are listed in the Yellow Pages, in the local Bar Association and online. (Note that not all "elder law" attorneys do complex tax planning.) While every attorney ought to be able to give you assistance in preparing the documents discussed in *Fore Talk*, elder law attorneys have the experience necessary for you to be confident in the *viability* of the documents they prepare.

*When I was executor of my brother's estate and the will was challenged, we were glad we had spent the time and money for an attorney to create and defend my brother's will. It was important to me for Ron's wishes to be carried out just as he wanted.*

# Creating your estate plan

When you need legal instruction—lawyers, of course, are prime sources—but knowledge gained (at $150-$250 an hour) can result in being smart, but broke. Fortunately, many lawyers will help you acquire a working knowledge of legal principles and procedures, but you need to study on your own. An estate plan includes a will, a Durable Power of Attorney for Finances, a Durable Power of Attorney for Health Care, and a Living Will. It may also include the creation of a trust.

# Why create a trust?

A trust document creates a legal entity to hold and control assets. The trust will define how you want the assets to be managed and distributed. A revocable trust is one whose terms can be changed during your lifetime and an irrevocable trust is one that usually cannot be changed.

Trusts can hold title to property and/or investment accounts and manage any other assets you wish to be managed on behalf of your heirs. The manager of a trust is called the trustee. However, because a trust can be very complicated and actually cost more to prepare than a will, it is an unnecessary expense unless the trust helps you accomplish certain goals. For example, some types of trusts can help save on taxes. A trust can keep your estate private. A trust can help reduce probate costs significantly if you own property in more than one state.

# The estate tax tango

There are a number of different kinds of trusts. Each one is designed to solve a specific problem. Trusts have tax consequences and need to be prepared by someone who understands this particular aspect of the law. A trust may provide for a disabled family member. It may also give you the peace of mind of knowing that your trustee can manage your property as you direct.

Until 2013, $5 million is exempt from the federal estate tax, with married couples able to shelter up to $10 million. The maximum tax rate on estates above that will be 35%—still a significant tax rate that can be especially difficult without cash on hand to take care of the tax liability.

> *"Unquestionably, there is progress. The average American now pays out twice as much in taxes as he formerly got in wages."*
>
> *– H.L. Mencken*

There are a number of ways to lower estate taxes. Individuals can give their children, relatives and others up to $5 million during their lifetimes without incurring federal gift taxes. Families also reduce the size of their taxable estates by giving money and other assets to charity. Reducing the size of your estate also lessens the expense of probate. Probate is a legal procedure that verifies the will, identifies, inventories and has appraisals on properties, pays debts and taxes, and distributes the remaining property as the will (or state law if there is no will) directs. Attorney fees for probate matters can range from 3% to 15% of your estate! Your attorney will know the fees.

# The trust question:
## *Is it for me?*

If you believe that your estate may be subject to estate taxes then you will find a trust a very flexible estate-planning tool. A charitable remainder trust can minimize capital gains taxes, provide you with an income and a charitable tax deduction, avoid gift and estate taxes, provide for minor children, children from a prior marriage, spouse, and heirs with special needs or even a pet as we learned from Leona Helmsley.

*Mrs. Helmsley, whose husband Harry owned hotels and a variety of other real estate, left a trust of $12 million to her Maltese, Trouble. The news that Trouble was the beneficiary of the largest bequest in her will caused such a stir that there were death threats against the dog. Heirs disputed the $5 billion estate and the court decided the dog would receive a $1 million award.*

Not everyone needs a trust. And even though you may have heard that a basic Revocable Living Trust is a simple document, trusts can be very complicated. This again is one of those times when you need to review the resources listed at the end of the book. Then have a talk with a knowledgeable estate planning attorney to decide what may be appropriate for you.

# Afterthought

The practice of law is an honored profession requiring years of study and experience. Understanding the complexity and application of the law can take a lifetime. Both federal law and state law are often a continually changing landscape. Finding a trusted legal advisor to help you prevent any difficulties in your estate planning will not only be a blessing to your family but may help you end restless days and anxious nights.

The law is very clear that you may write your own will. You can use forms or downloaded fill-in-the-blank guides to create all of your own estate-planning documents or write your will in your own words. But the likelihood of these documents being mis-stated, misquoted, contradictory, confusing and challenged is too great to risk.

Having a disinterested person to talk to at various times in our lives is something we all need. This is often the case when it comes to discussing your family and finances. People in your circle of friends have had the same difficulty and found an attorney that they trust and respect. That's why a referral is so important. There are a number of ways to get referrals; even calling the local bar association may be of help. Get familiar with the terms used in estate planning and with the documents; then find a competent and caring attorney.

All of the documents presented here will be well known to most estate planning attorneys. Your familiarity with these documents is designed to help you think through the answers that your attorney will need before you sit down and discuss your wishes and desires. While the attorney may listen and make suggestions, these are your decisions to make.

*"What did the lawyer name his daughter?"*
*"Sue!"*

# PRAYER

*Dear Heavenly Father, I am so grateful for the people that You have brought into my life—for my family, my friends and those closest to me. I'm also grateful for the professionals that You have brought into my life to provide help in those areas where I need advice. Thank You for the encouragement that comes from the religious and spiritual advisors I know. Thank You for the doctors whose knowledge and training has been so important to me and my family, and thank You for the wise counsel of attorneys who listen without judgment, act on my behalf and represent the best interests of those important to me. Teach me to not only hear but to respond in the most careful way to all of those who offer their help. May their guidance come as the leading of Your hand in my life. Guide me to discern the truth and may those who serve always represent only the best according to Your will.* AMEN

# Follow-up

| ATTORNEY REVIEW | |
|---|---|
| **Attorney #1:** | |
| Date contacted | Phone-office |
| Cell phone | Email |
| Attorney practice specialty | |
| Years of experience in estate planning | |
| Referred by | |
| Interview date | Phone or in person |
| Professionalism ☐ Y ☐ N | Knowledge ☐ Y ☐ N |
| Attitude ☐ Y ☐ N | Fee structure ☐ Y ☐ N |
| Compatibility ☐ Y ☐ N | Candidate ☐ Y ☐ N |

| Attorney #2: | |
|---|---|
| Date contacted | Phone-office |
| Cell phone | Email |
| Attorney practice specialty | |
| Years of experience in estate planning | |
| Referred by | |
| Interview date | Phone or in person |
| Professionalism ☐ Y ☐ N | Knowledge ☐ Y ☐ N |
| Attitude ☐ Y ☐ N | Fee structure ☐ Y ☐ N |
| Compatibility ☐ Y ☐ N | Candidate ☐ Y ☐ N |
| Attorney #3: | |
| Date contacted | Phone-office |
| Cell phone | Email |
| Attorney practice specialty | |
| Years of experience in estate planning | |
| Referred by | |
| Interview date | Phone or in person |
| Professionalism ☐ Y ☐ N | Knowledge ☐ Y ☐ N |
| Attitude ☐ Y ☐ N | Fee structure ☐ Y ☐ N |
| Compatibility ☐ Y ☐ N | Candidate ☐ Y ☐ N |

## PERSONAL ATTORNEYS

| My Personal Attorney #1: | |
|---|---|
| Name | Email |
| Address | |
| Phone | Cell phone |
| Services provided/specialty | |

| My Personal Attorney #2: | |
|---|---|
| Name | Email |
| Address | |
| Phone | Cell phone |
| Services provided/specialty | |

## YOUR CHECKLIST

| ☐ **Personal Will** | Date |
|---|---|
| Documents completed and signed ☐ Y ☐ N | |
| ☐ **Living Will** | Date |
| Documents completed and signed ☐ Y ☐ N | |
| ☐ **Durable Power of Attorney for Finances** | Date |
| Documents completed and signed ☐ Y ☐ N | |
| ☐ **Durable Power of Attorney for Health Care** | Date |
| Documents completed and signed ☐ Y ☐ N | |
| ☐ **Trusts** | Date |
| Documents completed and signed ☐ Y ☐ N | |

### Document Location

| Attorney's office ☐ Y ☐ N | Attorney's name |
|---|---|
| Address | |
| Locations of your personal copies | |
| Additional copies held by | |
| ☐ Documents reviewed by attorney | Date |

# The FIFTH *Critical Conversation:*
## How Can We Make a Personal Final Statement?

## CHAPTER SIX

Every time I say your name in prayer—which is practically all the time—I thank God for you, the God I worship with my whole life in the tradition of my ancestors. I miss you a lot, especially when I remember that last tearful good-bye, and I look forward to a joy-packed reunion. 2 TIMOTHY 1:3-4

And regarding the question, friends, that has come up about what happens to those already dead and buried, we don't want you in the dark any longer. First off, you must not carry on over them like people who have nothing to look forward to, as if the grave were the last word. Since Jesus died and broke loose from the grave, God will most certainly bring back to life those who died in Jesus. I THESSALONIANS 4:13-14

Goodbyes are never easy, but the pain of parting is much easier when we say, "See you this weekend…end of the semester…at Christmas."

Just knowing a "goodbye" is not final eases the sense of melancholy and loss. For Christians, death is not the end. Still, as the Bible reminds us, it is filled with sadness and sorrow. Even in Paul's letter to Timothy, he mentioned the tears shed at goodbyes. Changing the tears of pain to tears of promise and hope ought to be the goal of every Christian interment.

# The idea for
## *ForeTalk*

A few years ago, while I was serving as pastor of a church in North Carolina, my organist's mother passed away after a lingering illness. As I spoke with her, she said something I had seldom heard. "Before my mom became ill, we all had serious talks together; so when I go to meet my brothers and sisters at her funeral, it will be a time to celebrate Mom's thoughtfulness."

When I asked her to tell me about her mother's talks, here's what she shared with me:

- **Her will**
  "My mother wrote her will some time ago. She gave each of us all a copy and discussed it with us."

- **Possessions**
  "She asked if there were any personal items that we would like to have from her household. She told us that she would like us to take them and, if more than one of us wanted the same item, we could talk it over together."

- **Health care directive**
  "She had written her health care directive and a Living Will and explained it to us. For her, being kept alive was not the same as being alive."

- **Funeral planning**
  "She had completely planned her funeral. She showed us the dress that she wanted to wear and her plans for the service. She had already paid for the burial site. She had selected her casket and paid for all the funeral expenses. She had selected all of the music, the Bible passages,

NOTES

and even the speakers, pallbearers, and honorary pallbearers. We're not going back to any worry or burden; we are all just going to hug each other and be thankful for Mom."

Now you know where the idea for *ForeTalk* came from. She had not only thought about her future beFORE this expected event occurred, she TALKed about it and took action—foretalk.

## A look ahead

- **The difference between a funeral and memorial service**
- **The difference between a traditional funeral and direct burial**
- **Burial or cremation?**
- **Planning your own funeral or memorial service**
- **The expense of the exit**
- **Giving the gift of life**

# The difference between a funeral and memorial service

**A funeral** is a ceremony, or perhaps even a series of ceremonies, marking a person's life by recalling the experiences that live on in the memories of their families and loved ones.

In North America, a funeral is typically held within three days of a person's death and usually includes more than a final ceremony.

### *Funeral traditions*

- A visitation may be held at a funeral home or at the home of the deceased the day before the funeral service to allow time for family or friends to travel. Those unable to attend the funeral are able to express their condolences during the visitation.
- A funeral service is often held at a funeral home, a church, or the home of the deceased.
- A burial ceremony or interment is a brief service at the graveside.
- The deceased's casket is usually present at the funeral. It may be open or closed.
- A wake, or gathering, frequently follows the funeral.

**A wake** is a tradition from the days when the body lay in the casket at home prior to burial. Someone was always with the casket containing the body and people usually stayed awake all night. This was a time of praying, eating, drinking, remembering and sharing details about the life of the person whose body lay in the casket.

Today, in North America, a wake is a gathering that usually follows the funeral or the burial ceremony and can be held in any preferred location. Often food is prepared by family and friends. This gathering provides a time for reflection, comfort and encouragement for loved ones and a time to renew friendships.

**A memorial** is similar to a funeral service except for its timing and the absence of a casket. The comforting messages that are central to a religious funeral service tend to be optional in a memorial service. A memorial service is just that—a time to remember.

## *Characteristics of a memorial service*

- A memorial service may be held at any time after the death of a loved one. Because the casket or urn is not usually present, the service may be held weeks or months after the burial or cremation.
- A memorial service may be held anywhere the family chooses. It may follow a funeral or burial in another city or state.
- Sharing a meal together may or may not be part of a memorial service.
- A memorial service need not be religious in nature.
- A memorial service is appropriate following a direct burial or direct cremation. (See definitions that follow.)

NOTES

# The difference between a traditional funeral and direct burial

**A traditional full-service funeral** offers complete services by the funeral provider and is the most expensive type of funeral. It usually includes a viewing or visitation and formal funeral service, use of a hearse to transport the body to the funeral and burial site, and burial, entombment, or cremation. The professional services of the funeral director can be valuable guidance.

## Included in a full-service funeral

- Copies of death certificate
- Purchase of a casket
- Embalming and dressing the body (perhaps the purchase of a dress or suit)
- Services of a hairstylist and cosmetician
- Rental of the funeral home for the visitation and service itself
- Services of clergy and musicians.
- Use of limousines to transport the family and pallbearers
- A graveside service

**Direct burial** is less expensive than a traditional full-service burial because fewer funeral home services are required.

## Included in a direct burial

- Burial shortly after death, usually in a simple casket
- No embalming if no viewing or visitation is involved
- No rental for funeral home because no funeral services are held
- Funeral home's basic services fees
- Transportation and care of the body
- Basic casket or burial container

If the family chooses to go to the cemetery for the burial, the funeral home charges a fee for a graveside service, often referred to as "opening and closing the grave."

**Direct cremation,** like direct burial, also costs less than a traditional full-service funeral.

## Included in a direct cremation

- Cremation of the body shortly after death without embalming

- Remains placed in an urn or other container
- No viewing or visitation involved, although a memorial service may be held with or without the cremated remains present
- Funeral home's fees for basic services
- Transportation and care of the body

A crematory may be included or, if the funeral home doesn't own the crematory, the fee for this service may be additional. There is typically a charge for purchasing an urn or other container.

**Be sure to tell family members about the plans you've made and where your documents (such as those at the end of this chapter) are filed.** If they aren't aware that you've made funeral or memorial plans, your wishes may not be carried out. And if they don't know you've prepaid the funeral costs, they could end up paying for the same arrangements needlessly.

# Burial or cremation?

Over the last decade, cremation has become a viable alternative for many families for economic reasons. However, in some communities, especially in the south and midwest of the United States, burial tends to be the only option considered by most families.

**Burial** means the body is interred—perhaps in a mausoleum or a vault in the ground or even at sea. Christian theology and tradition teaches bodily resurrection; therefore, most Christians choose burial over cremation. Imitating Jesus, they choose burial because the body of Jesus was placed in a (borrowed) tomb. Early Christians

NOTES

were also laid to rest with the body intact in catacombs, graves, or tombs. From the time when churches were first constructed in Europe and America, it was the custom to build a cemetery near a church. As you travel across rural America, you see countless beautiful churches that have cemeteries alongside them. That's where the faithful have been buried for decades. Interestingly, it has been a custom to bury the body facing east, the direction from which Jesus is said to return.

In the United States and other countries, visiting the graves of loved ones provides a way to remember their lives and celebrate the contributions they made to family, friends, and society. Memorial Day, also known as Remembrance Day or Decoration Day, has been a traditional time to visit graves in the U.S.

In the Old Testament, burial was common for the patriarchs and their families. Jewish tradition favored burial over cremation because they believed that being burned by fire was a punishment reserved for evildoers. In the past, burial was the only official option for Roman Catholics.

Burial may require the purchase of a casket as well as a vault for the casket if it's placed in the ground. Having a burial plot or aboveground mausoleum adds to the expense.

**Cremation** (or incineration) refers to the burning of the body after death, one of mankind's oldest ways of disposing of a body. War and disease often necessitated the burning of corpses.

Because the Romans burned their dead, Christians associated cremation with pagan beliefs and practices. Many Christians still consider it a pagan practice. Once a seldom-chosen means for dealing with a body in North America, the practice of cremation has grown in popularity because it typically costs one-third to one-half of what a burial costs.

In addition, cremation involves fewer services from the funeral home or undertaker. In many instances, an urn with ashes is simply kept at a loved one's home. Some choose to scatter the remains in a place that's meaningful to the family and the deceased. (It is usually appropriate to get permission before scattering the ashes.)

Even though cremation is less expensive than a burial, it's not a simple process. The furnace must reach 1400°-2000° F and can take 90 minutes or more for a body to be completely incinerated. Afterwards, the remains (bones) are ground to uniform size and placed in an urn along with the ashes.

**At present, the Roman Catholic Church as well as most other Christian**

denominations have no prohibition against cremation. However, Christian theology, Biblical practice, and tradition clearly favor burial over cremation.

The burial site for the casket or urn is an expense to be aware of. No matter what your plans for the body, prepaying for the burial site may be a wise idea, especially as we get older. The short time available between death and burial usually doesn't allow enough time for your family to compare costs and, in many cases, discuss where the remains are to be placed.

**If cremation is your choice, why not donate your body to medical research?** If you live in or near a city with a medical research facility, a university, or a medical college, your gift will be a meaningful act of generosity and may be of significant value to solving problems of aging or disease. Bodies are treated with care and the remains cremated.

An article in *The Wall Street Journal* has recognized the University of Indiana School of Medicine for requesting full details on a donor, including a photo and biography. This not only honors the generosity of the donor but also teaches the students more about having compassion for those in their care. Both the students and the families praised the new policy. Rita Borrelli, whose husband donated his body, said, "It gave me some needed closure because of the respect they showed my husband."[15]

**This is a no-cost option that may make your death more meaningful to those who come after you.** It also adds value to your passing. Be sure your family knows your wishes and you have notified the medical school.

97

# Planning your own funeral or memorial service

A funeral or memorial ought to be one of the most personal times a family can share. But without planning, it can be more painful, expensive, overwrought, and distressing to every family member. In contrast, **a funeral service planned well in advance can take away much of the stress and pain facing a family after the death of a loved one.** Sadly, only a few individuals think ahead and plan their own funeral or memorial.

Planning can avoid embarrassment and confusion for your loved ones. Occasionally the person conducting the funeral doesn't even know the deceased. Here's an example of what could happen.

A bereaved Kentucky wife and 10-year-old son were sitting near the casket at her late husband's funeral. The preacher droned on about the many fine qualities of the deceased. As he went on to describe the sensitive husband, caring father, generous humanitarian, she couldn't stand it any longer. She nudged her son and whispered, "Go on up there and see who's in that casket. That's sure not your daddy he's talkin' about!"

## What to include when planning your service

- The type of service to be conducted
- The place and time of day
- Favorite hymns or music to be played
- Vocalists or instrumentalists
- Favorite Biblical passages, poems, or readings
- Pallbearers and honorary pallbearers
- Burial clothing selection
- A casket or urn you prefer
- Items to be placed in the casket
- Distinctive decorations, flowers, or wreaths
- Your preference on how the wake or celebration of life should be conducted, including special foods, beverages, sweets, or snacks that have a personal meaning
- Special friends or groups you may wish to be present
- Your obituary
- Your selection of someone to lead the service (e.g., pastor, priest, minister)

There is no limit to the details that can be written out when planning a funeral or memorial. In fact, **the more details, the easier it will be for the family to carry out your wishes**.

Unusual requests are becoming increasingly more common. Want your casket pulled to the cemetery by a Harley motorcycle hearse? Easy. Ditch somber hymns for a so-hot-it's-cool jazz band? Done. Think your loved ones should keep you close at hand? LifeGem compresses cremated remains, converting the carbon into actual diamonds for setting into a ring, necklace, or earrings.[16]

Sad and somber services of the past are being replaced by celebrations of life in which humor, fun, and laughter prevail. Your careful, thoughtful planning expressing your choices will mean more than you know to your family and loved ones.

Use the forms at the end of this chapter as a guide to planning your service. Remember, if you don't plan it, someone else will. Who better to do this than you?

# The expense of the exit

Planning and prepaying a funeral can often save substantial amounts of money if you shop for quality services at the lowest price. It is not uncommon for members bereaved family to spend far more on a funeral than necessary to visibly demonstrate their love and respect. When family members feel vulnerable and grief stricken, planning your funeral can lead to uninformed and unwarranted decisions they may later regret. Giving an elaborate send-off can be seen as a substitute for the love and attention they may not have expressed well during your lifetime. In truth, love and respect is best seen in the faces and embraces of the friends and loved ones who come to visit the family. **Planning your own service also reflects your budget preferences. It is possible to spend more money on**

**a funeral than on a new car or the down payment of a home.** No doubt, you can think of places you would prefer the money be spent rather than on an elaborate funeral or casket. And for many families, the increasing expenses of a funeral combined with the rising costs of either a burial or cremation can be a serious cause for concern.

In 1963, Jessica Milford wrote *The American Way of Death,*[17] an alarming, funny, sad commentary on the funeral industry of that time. This book sparked such an extensive review of funeral home practices that many states as well as the federal government enacted laws to protect the consumer.

While the laws vary from state to state, pay attention to the basics.

## *Recognizing your rights*

- You have the right to choose the funeral goods and services you want. This includes embalming, which is not required unless viewing is requested.
- If state or local law requires you to buy any particular item, the funeral provider must disclose it on the price list, with a reference to the specific law.
- You may buy a casket anywhere you choose and the funeral provider may not refuse or charge a fee to handle a casket you bought elsewhere.
- A funeral provider that offers cremation must make alternative containers available.

A burial vault, though not required for the protection of the casket, is generally required by the cemetery to prevent a sinking or depression in the ground over time.

**The most expensive item in most funerals is the casket. That is the reason funeral homes are required to allow you to purchase a casket elsewhere, or even rent one.**

You may want to shop for a casket online. By researching casket prices, you will be a much better-equipped consumer when you visit your funeral provider. Caskets may be purchased wholesale in many cities and are easily found on the Internet. Savings can be as high as 80% and free one-day delivery is often included in the price. In fact, you may find that you can lower your casket expense by simply knowing what a casket can cost and discussing the pricing with the funeral director.

It is a little known fact that a casket can be rented. If you wish a casket to be present at the service, it can be done without a costly purchase. Each rental has a new interior for every use. Remember, no casket or embalming technique can protect a body indefinitely. A casket does not preserve a body; it's simply a convenient means to move it from one place to another.

**Consider planning and prepaying for your funeral as a gift of comfort, peace of mind and relief that you can give members of your family. The gratitude for your thoughtfulness will be a lasting legacy in itself.**

**If you are a veteran,** you have certain burial benefits, but they do not come automatically. They must be requested. Preplanning is required. If you are retired from the military, disabled due to a service-related injury, die in a VA facility or are currently under VA contract for care, then you may qualify. The benefits include burial in a military cemetery, a headstone, honor guard, and flag. There is no opening or closing the gravesite expense for being buried at a military cemetery. If you do not wish to be in a military cemetery, there is currently a $300 burial expense allowance. Your funeral service provider should be knowledgeable and helpful in explaining the complete program for veterans.

# Giving the gift of life

Being an organ donor can be a wonderful act of generosity and a momentous gift to enhance or even save the life of another human being. While some believe it is preferable for organ donations to come from young people in good health, that is not always true. Advancing age is not a reason to shy away from being a donor. The medical team involved can evaluate donor requests and determine which organs are practical for transplant. **However, be sure to write down your wishes and let your family and your doctor know you want to be a donor.**

By donating your organs, you can save or improve as many as 50 lives. And many families say that knowing their loved one helped save other lives helped them cope with their loss.

At the time of this writing, more than 110,000 people—enough to populate a town the size of Clearwater, Florida—are awaiting a transplant in the United States.

# The most important time

In his excellent book *Last Rights,* Stephen P. Kiernan provides four final lessons for the end of life. The fourth lesson reminds us that awareness of our approaching death can make this time one of the most beautiful periods in our lives.

*"The fourth and final lesson is the lesson of the leaves. In fall's bright colors nature makes it clear: the most important time in your life is not the moment of your death but the time as it approaches." [18]*

We know the future. Death is approaching every one of us—both young and old, good health or poor. It cannot be avoided, but it can be anticipated.

**One important way to make our lives a blessing for our families and loved ones is to remove anxiety and fear during these most important days.**

And now I have a word
for you who brashly announce,
"Today—at the latest,
tomorrow—we're off
to such and such a city for the year.
We're going to start a business
and make a lot of money."
You don't know the first
thing about tomorrow.
You're nothing but a wisp
of fog, catching a brief bit
of sun before disappearing.
Instead, make it a habit to say,
"If the Master wills it and we're
still alive, we'll do this or that."
JAMES 4:13-15

So teach us to number our days,
that we may apply our hearts
unto wisdom.
PSALMS 90:12 KJV

While our days are limited, there is no limitation on the quality of life we put into those days. To apply our hearts wisely doesn't mean sitting and waiting for the grim reaper to appear. Planning adds to the quality of today and tomorrow. You have no idea what a planned service can mean to your family and friends. Make the time. Make a great last impression.

## *Practicing foretalk means taking action*

- Talk with your loved ones and plan your response and actions before illness, incapacity or death occurs.
- Discuss end-of-life issues honestly, without fear or discomfort.
- Understand that death is a part of living.
- Remove the stressful uncertainty and hasty decisions left to many families when they are least

able to deal with them.

**Thoughtful preparation can enrich the lives of our loved ones by our day-to-day practice of foretalk. The time spent will be some of the very best hours and minutes we can give on their behalf. These days are like the beautiful days of fall when our anticipation of the future can be bright colors instead of the somber and dreary days that await those who fail to exercise the privilege of meaningful conversation before death arrives.**

What a God we have!
And how fortunate we are to have him,
this Father of our Master Jesus!
Because Jesus was raised from the dead,
we've been given a brand-new life and have
everything to live for, including a future in
heaven—and the future starts now! God is
keeping careful watch over us and the future.
The Day is coming when you'll have it
all—life healed and whole.

1 PETER 1:3-5

# Afterthought

This chapter has primarily dealt with planning what you would like to happen after your death. Burial or cremation, a funeral or memorial service, where to be buried are all decisions that you, not someone else, should be making. Taking the time to plan your own funeral may sound a bit strange but, in reality, it is a wonderful example of showing your love by having foretalk.

*"You should always go to other people's funerals,*
*otherwise they won't come to yours."*
*—Yogi Berra*

The law guarantees specific rights when it comes to knowing and understanding all of your funeral expenses. It also means you have choices to make regarding what kind of funeral or memorial service you prefer. Leaving these decisions for your family to make during the period of bereavement may not only be costly but, in some ways, unkind. Your state laws and the policies and practices of funeral homes need to be understood and your preferences need to be made clear.

There are a number of ways to do funeral planning. (The chapter that follows addresses pre-paid funerals and for whom they are most appropriate.)

One of the most meaningful decisions you can make is to extend the life of another by being an organ donor or donating your body to a medical facility for research. With organ donation, the body can be returned for burial and an open casket will still be possible if that is desired. Donating your body to a medical school is a positive and compassionate form of cremation that honors our creator as well as the donor.

Thinking over your funeral service will give you the opportunity to reflect on some of the most significant experiences of your life. Recalling friends and family, some not seen in years, and determining what role you may want them to play at your funeral or memorial service can be extremely rewarding.

To be asked to serve in any role in your funeral service or memorial can be a great honor, especially when those asked know they were chosen specifically by you.

Make this service a celebration by choosing the elements that best reflect your life, the special events and loved ones most meaningful to you. Take the time right now to plan your own service and make it as personal as your fingerprint. You have no idea what this can mean to those who attend and especially to those you love.

Use the forms and the follow-up section to start the process. Writing down your thoughts is the key to making your passing easier for everyone in bereavement.

## PRAYER

*Dear Creator Father,* thank You for all that has been meaningful in my life. For the love I have known, freely given and freely received from family, work, friends and faith. May my final message to those who mean the most to me affirm my gratitude, my love and my life as gifts from You. Let this passing be a reminder to all that the gift of eternal life is ours to claim and celebrate through Jesus our Lord. AMEN

But let me tell you something wonderful, a mystery I'll probably never fully understand. We're not all going to die—but we are all going to be changed. You hear a blast to end all blasts from a trumpet, and in the time that you look up and blink your eyes—it's over. On signal from that trumpet from heaven, the dead will be up and out of their graves, beyond the reach of death, never to die again. At the same moment and in the same way, we'll all be changed. In the resurrection scheme of things, this has to happen: everything perishable taken off the shelves and replaced by the imperishable, this mortal replaced by the immortal...Thank God!

I CORINTHIANS 15:51-53

# Follow-Up

## My preferences regarding my funeral or memorial service

| Name | Date |
|---|---|
| Social Security Number | Military ID |

| Other important ID numbers, passwords, logins, email addresses | |
|---|---|
| | |
| | |
| | |

☐ I am an organ donor.

☐ I have donated my body to this medical school.

☐ I am a veteran and would like to use my veteran's recognition, flag and honor guard, and have contacted the Veterans Administration regarding my request.

☐ I prefer to use this funeral home, church, chapel, hall or facility:

| Name | Phone |
|---|---|
| Address | |

☐ I prefer burial in this military cemetery:

| Name | Phone |
|---|---|
| Address | |

☐ I have prepaid my funeral expense:

| Where? | Phone |
|---|---|
| Address | |

☐ To cover funeral expenses, I have an insurance policy with:

| Name | Phone |
|---|---|
| Amount | |

☐ I prefer a funeral service *(casket present, service held shortly after my death).*

☐ I prefer cremation following the funeral service.

☐ I prefer direct cremation/burial with a memorial service to follow at a convenient time chosen by my family.

☐ I have no preferences for the funeral or memorial service.

☐ I have the following preferences for my funeral/memorial service:

**Family and/or friends I would like to speak:**

| Name | Phone | Contacted ☐ |
|---|---|---|
| Name | Phone | Contacted ☐ |

**Those I would like to preside at the service (clergy, priests, etc.):**

| Name | Phone | Contacted ☐ |
|---|---|---|
| Name | Phone | Contacted ☐ |

**Those I would like to serve as pallbearers:**

| Name | Phone | Contacted ☐ |
|---|---|---|
| Name | Phone | Contacted ☐ |

**Honorary pallbearers:**

| Name | Phone | Contacted ☐ |
|---|---|---|
| Name | Phone | Contacted ☐ |

**I prefer the service to be** ☐ *fun* ☐ *humorous* ☐ *light* ☐ *dignified* ☐ *quiet* ☐ *serious* ☐ *somber*

**I prefer my casket to be** ☐ *open* ☐ *closed*

**My favorite Scripture passages, poems, literature selections that I would like to have included in the service:**

**In lieu of flowers I would like memorial gifts to be sent to:**

☐ I prefer a wake (gathering) following the funeral or memorial.

☐ I would like the following at my wake (food, beverages, flowers, photos, music, etc...):

**My preferred place for burial is:**

| City | Cemetery |
|------|----------|

**My preferred place for my scattering ashes following cremation is:**

☐ *Buried* ☐ *Scattering Garden* ☐ *Niche* ☐ *Cremation Garden* ☐ *Container*

☐ *Other:*

**My preferred place for my ashes to be interred:**

| City | Cemetery |
|------|----------|

☐ I have prepaid my burial site.

*Cemetery*

| Address | City |
|---------|------|

☐ I would like a headstone or grave marker.

☐ I have selected and prepaid my headstone or marker from:

| Company | City |
|---------|------|

*Location of documentation/receipts:*

☐ I would prefer to have this passage or inscription on the marker:

☐ Here are suggestions for what to include in my obituary:
( *Be smart, write your own obituary.*)

*(You may include anything you wish: your education, work and other significant experiences, hobbies, friends or organizations you wish to recognize, memberships, honors received, military experience, relationships—spouse(s), children, grandchildren and great-grandchildren.)*

☐ My obituary should be placed in these newspapers :

*Please note: Newspapers' charges vary by newspaper but all charge by the word and charge extra for an added photo. This can be expensive. The cost can easily reach $1000 or more.*

Family and friends who should be contacted following my death:

| Name | Phone |
|------|-------|
| *Name* | *Phone* |
| *Name* | *Phone* |
| *Name* | *Phone* |
| *Name* | *Phone* |

Churches or religious organizations to notify:

Military organizations to notify:

Unions or fraternal organizations to notify:

Alumni organizations to notify:

Additional notes *(Items to be placed in the casket, or any specific requests or thoughts, etc.)*:

**Give copies of this document to members of your family and have additional ones made for your funeral or memorial service provider. Add additional pages as you wish.**

Careful planning puts you ahead in the long run;
hurry and scurry puts you further behind.  PROVERBS 21:5

The rich think their wealth protects them;
they imagine themselves safe behind it.  PROVERBS 18:11-12

*Insurance is the only purchase that
you must make when you don't need it,
because when you need it, you can't buy it.*

What we are willing to risk reveals what we value. No one wants to leave his or her family at risk. The loss of a parent, a bread winner or caregiver is a tragic occurrence. Financially, it can deprive children of an education and leave a crushing burden of debt. Later in life, our insurance needs change but they don't disappear. In fact, in some ways they become even more important—perhaps to provide income protection for a surviving spouse, estate and/or legacy planning.

Home and automobile insurance, health insurance and life insurance are all designed to minimize the risk of loss. We recognize homeowners and automobile insurance as part of the cost of ownership. However, when it comes to protecting our family's well being with life insurance, many who ought to be insured are not insured at all.

Long term care insurance is a fairly new type of insurance that grew out of the aging baby boomer market. Burial insurance has been available for some time but is still unfamiliar to many. Because of the importance of insurance to foretalk, this chapter is one to read carefully.

# Looking ahead

- **A life insurance primer**
- **The annuity option**
- **Long term care insurance**
- **Burial insurance**
- **A Totten Trust**

# A life insurance primer

*"Fun is like life insurance; the older you get, the more it costs." – Kin Hubbard*

**One third of the American adult population do not carry life insurance. But when it comes to baby boomers (those born following World War II—between 1946 and 1964), more than 72% have life insurance.**[19] Boomers grew up with insurance and know that it's easier and less expensive to buy life insurance when you're young. To ensure that the interests of your loved ones will not be undermined financially by your death, you should understand the various types of life insurance, starting with basically two types.

## Temporary insurance

Temporary life insurance is frequently called "term" because it provides coverage for a specified length of time or a specified term. As pure insurance, it often has no benefits beyond paying out a predetermined sum at the time of your death. If the term expires before you do, the coverage can expire. Many term policies change into annually renewable term policies (ART). A number of different

types of term insurance policies exist. And because they offer pure protection with no investment options or guaranteed insurability, they are less expensive than permanent policies. Be aware that the premium you pay can increase as you get older, and you may be required to take medical exams at the time of renewal.

### There are 2 subcategories:

Level Term means that the death benefit stays the same throughout the term but premiums may increase over time.

Decreasing Term means that the death benefit decreases with time (usually yearly), but the premium may remain the same. The premiums vary with the amount and term (or time) of coverage.

# Permanent insurance

Permanent life insurance is known as whole life insurance. In addition to the insurance protection, whole life insurance sets aside a part of your premium into a tax-deferred reserve account or cash value account that can grow in value as years pass. This investment account may be paid out to you as a lump sum or over time. Typically, the premium, cash value and the death benefits are guaranteed for the life of the policy. Whole life premiums are typically less costly when you're younger because you have less risk of death. Buying a new whole life policy can become very expensive as you get older.

Permanent life also offers variations such as Universal Life (UL) and Variable Universal Life (VUL). Universal Life combines both temporary and permanent insurance benefits. Variable Universal Life invests a portion of your premium in stock market indexes or other investment selections (called subaccounts). This results in a variable cash value. But many policies now have a minimum guaranteed return.

**Why would you choose permanent life insurance instead of temporary? The main advantage is that you don't have to die to get a return on your investment.** Plus your insurance cannot be canceled—it's permanent. It will continue no matter the changes in your health. And no medical exams are required after the initial purchase. In times of economic chaos, the investment portion may be a wise supplement to your other investments.

Rob and Kathy Bryant each owned a paid-up permanent life policy which they had purchased years ago. When Rob passed away, the policy paid off a small mortgage, paid all the funeral expenses, and left a legacy gift that benefited their five grandchildren. The beneficiaries of Kathy's policy, the five grandchildren, will have a major portion of college expenses covered. *"Without the insurance,"* Kathy says, *"our life savings would not have been enough to take care of my financial needs. It (life insurance) did not seem like much at the time but it was a great benefit when I needed it."*

Everyone has different insurance needs. It's important to talk with a life insurance agent who can adequately explain the differences between the various life insurance policies and products available in today's market. **If you currently own life insurance, the changes in the kinds of insurance offered, as well as the investment selections and availability of global investments, make reviewing your insurance options more important than ever.** Remember, the ability of insurance to create an income when the chief breadwinner can no longer provide or the children's caretaker can no longer care for the children can be an incalculable value.

## *Life insurance is important if you have any of the following:*

- A spouse, children, relatives, or any other dependents
- A special-needs child or relative
- A mortgage or other large debts
- A complex estate with a potential tax bill
- Business debt or a business partnership
- A charity, church, college, or other institution you want to assist financially
- Any individuals other than your spouse or children to whom you want to leave money when you die

*"I don't want to tell you how much insurance I carry with the Prudential, but all I can say is: when I go, they go too." – Jack Benny*

**With a valid reason, there is no limit to the amount of life insurance you can purchase. However, it's important to be clear on all of the fees, the commissions, and possible penalties for withdrawal of your money (the liquidity of your insurance policy investment).** It is also important to know exactly how the benefits will be paid to your beneficiaries. Do you want lump sum payments or payouts over time? You must specify your wishes and have them clearly expressed in the life insurance contract you sign. Don't be afraid to ask questions and get understandable answers.

For those whose estate will owe federal taxes, determining who owns your life insurance policy is very important. If you are the owner of the policy (the one who pays the premiums), then the proceeds are included in your federally taxable estate. If someone else owns the policy (e.g., an irrevocable trust), the proceeds of your policy would not be included in your estate.

If your estate will not be subject to taxation under federal law, then there's less need to be concerned. However, if it is subject to be taxed, you may want to transfer ownership of the policy. This involves potentially complex discussions, so be sure to talk with your attorney and tax advisor as well as your insurance agent.

The billionaire Malcolm Forbes purchased life insurance policies to cover the taxes on his estate—*Forbes Magazine* and the associated businesses he owned. Because of his planning, his family inherited the company and did not have to liquidate the business in order to pay taxes on the estate. The life insurance payout covered all the taxes due.

Similarly, if there is an appreciated asset in your estate (e.g., a business, farmland, or other property valued in the millions of dollars), life insurance can be a significant resource for paying taxes due. Again, talk to your agent.

Additionally, because life insurance has a stated beneficiary, life insurance proceeds will avoid probate and pass directly to your beneficiary.

> *"If a man doesn't believe in life insurance, let him die once without it. That will teach him a lesson."*
> *– Will Rogers*

As you can see, including your insurance professional in your list of trusted advisors adds a valuable resource for you and your family.

# The annuity option

Life insurance transfers the financial risk of your death to an insurance company.

An annuity transfers the risk of outliving your income to an insurance company. In other words, life insurance provides financial protection from an early death. An annuity provides protection against living too long. Guaranteed income for life is a significant financial benefit.

**An annuity is simply a regular payment—monthly, quarterly or annually—paid out to you. In exchange for your upfront payment, the insurance company guarantees a steady stream of payments for life or for a specified number of years.**

If you have a pension plan, that's a form of an annuity. Over time, you pay money into a pension plan so, during your retirement, portions of that payment are returned to you in increments.

In fact, you could consider Social Security a form of an annuity (some would add "with less security"). Social Security collects payments over your working life and deposits them into a Social Security fund. When you retire, the fund pays out a benefit to you (at least, that is the plan).

In an annuity contract, you determine how much to deposit and when and how long your payments will occur. Annuities can be purchased by installment premiums or by a single premium. When paid by a single premium, benefits may begin immediately or be deferred. Your income payout may last as long as you live, or you may select a joint life option so your payout can continue being paid to your spouse.

**A major advantage of a life annuity is that it provides an income that cannot be outlived.**

## Get acquainted with an annuity

- An annuity is a contract sold by an insurance company that guarantees a specified income for the rest of your life and, if you choose, for the life of your spouse.
- Tax deferred annuities allow the returns to accumulate over time and may pay out a higher rate of return when annuitization or income distribution begins.
- Tax deferred annuities may be either fixed or variable.
- Annuities can be a supplemental retirement income plan.
- The return can depend upon the type of investment chosen as well as the type of payouts selected.
- Annuities are usually purchased with a lump-sum payment. Investments can be fixed or variable.
- Fixed annuities specify their fixed rates of return in advance. Your principal and a minimum rate of return are guaranteed.
- Variable annuities will pay based on the returns of the investments selected from a number of options.
- An equity-indexed annuity combines both fixed and variable annuities by offering an investment minimum guarantee as well as a link to an investment index.

Annuity contracts have certain tax advantages that are beneficial. Annuity deposits, payments, or purchases are usually made with after-tax dollars. The accumulation, growth or income inside the annuity will be tax deferred. When the payout of the annuity begins, a portion will be taxable at your current tax rate.

Knowing that your annuity income will continue as long as you live and, if you specify, continue as long as your spouse lives, can be a relief when planning for the future. A "lifetime guaranteed pay annuity" (names may vary) commits the insurance company to continue payments for either the stated guaranteed period or the rest of your life, whichever is longer. Typically, the guaranteed period is 10 or 20 years (measured from when you started receiving annuity payments). The payments will continue after your death to one or more beneficiaries until the guaranteed period concludes.

There are a wide variety of annuity contracts available from a number of sources including financial service firms and insurance companies. An insurance company, however, issues every contract.

**Annuities are complicated. It is important to know about the sales charges (sometimes called the "load"), how they are paid, and what fees are included in the contract.**

The concept of liquidity—that is, when you can withdraw all or some of your principal—needs to be clearly explained.

Some annuities permit annual withdrawals of 5%-15% of your investment with no sales charge penalty.

Those in a preretirement category (50-65 years old) most often purchase **deferred annuities.** A deferred annuity will delay your payout until retirement (or whenever you choose to have your payments begin). Those close to or in retirement often purchase **immediate annuities**, and payments can begin in the year of purchase.

**With corporations revising pension plans, social security benefits being under pressure, and 401(k) and IRA accounts experiencing drops in value with each stock market decline, annuities may offer a more secure retirement and become a significant part of a complete retirement plan.**

# Long term care insurance

"Given a choice, most people prefer to die in their own homes—another option seldom covered by Medicaid. Purchasing long term care insurance with the right benefits means that you can decide where you will receive care while protecting your life savings."[20]

Long term care insurance (LTC) is a relatively new type of insurance. It is designed to make payments to a nursing home or other facility when you become disabled or unable to care for yourself.

Some say everyone needs long term care insurance; however, many adults with assets of a million dollars or more choose to self-insure. And although not everyone will spend time in a nursing home or long term care facility, if that's required, it can quickly run up large bills. The length of time, the type of care needed, and the quality of care or facility can run the costs into tens of thousands of dollars very quickly. Long term care policies usually cover costs up to a maximum policy amount.

**Remember, the purpose of insurance is to reduce risk.** The time to consider long term care insurance is preretirement, perhaps as early as age 50. The younger you are, the more remote your risk of needing long term care so the premiums are priced low. The risk of being in a nursing home or other skilled care facility increases and the cost of long term care insurance goes higher with each birthday. How much you pay for this type of policy depends on your age, your health, and the benefits you want it to provide.

**Medicare, after a REQUIRED 3-night minimum hospital stay, will pay in full only for the first 20 days of skilled care.** For days 21 up to day 100, you pay your own expenses up to $144.50 per day at this writing (2012), and Medicare pays any balance left. All payments after day 100 are your responsibility. Medicaid participants must spend down assets in order to qualify for continuing care.

Rate increases will continue because Americans keep living longer and a lingering illness is more probable than experiencing sudden death. These statistics tell the story: In 1994, 7.3 million Americans needed long-term care (LTC) services at an average cost of nearly $43,800 per year per person. By 2000, this number rose to 9 million Americans at nearly $55,750 per year. In 2010, it was near $75,000 per year. By 2030, the number of people needing LTC will skyrocket to 23+ million, with projected long-term care costs reaching $300,000 annually per individual![21]

Long term care insurance can pay for care in your home, in an assisted living facility, or 24-hour care in a nursing home, depending on your policy. Some policies exclude specific conditions such as certain forms of cancer, diabetes, or mental illness and nervous disorders. Some may require a hospital stay before benefits begin and others won't cover any pre-existing conditions. Here again, talk to a trusted insurance professional for advice.

**With the rising costs of health care, buying long term care insurance may be smart.** If you choose LTC insurance, be sure that your premium doesn't exceed 3% to 7% of your current monthly income. You can quickly spend yourself poor as premiums rise over time. However, for a somewhat higher premium, there may be LTC policies that have a paid-in-full feature available.

To get more information on long term care insurance, review the websites listed in the internet resources section and see an agent who specializes in LTC insurance.

# Burial insurance

**What is commonly called burial insurance is actually a life insurance policy to cover funeral expenses.** There are two types: a policy purchased from an agent that *can be used* to cover burial costs, and one purchased from a funeral home to cover specific funeral expenses selected in advance.

## Specific purpose policy

There are numerous ads on television offering insurance for final expenses. These temporary policies are usually sold with limited values from $5,000 to $25,000. They usually don't require medical exams, can be purchased up to age 80 and can provide coverage until age 100. The American Association of Retired Persons (AARP) offers a number of final expense life policies from insurance suppliers. One example is a $15,000 policy called Guaranteed Acceptance Life Insurance (www.aarp.org) where the proceeds are paid to a beneficiary to cover the cost of a loved one's funeral.

If you are in good health, buying a life insurance policy from an insurance agent may be a preferred alternative since the amount can be larger (usually beginning at $25,000) and may be less expensive based on the amount of insurance.

Be aware, though, that it's possible you could leave $25,000 for funeral expenses and have the beneficiary choose cremation and an inexpensive funeral, pocketing the differ-

ence. (Purchasing a sports car may be perceived as a better investment than a casket.) However, you can specify that any money in excess of the actual expenses be given to your church or favorite charity.

# Prepaid funeral insurance

**The second form of insurance is a prepaid funeral policy purchased from a funeral home. It will pay for a funeral anytime in the future at today's costs no matter how expenses rise over time. The funeral home is the beneficiary.** The policy amount is guaranteed to cover the services you select, no matter the costs at the time of death. Inflation protection can make this type of policy an attractive option and allows you to make you own choices and pay years in advance.

Funeral expenses can vary from $3500 to over $25,000, with the average cost being approximately $9500 at the time of this writing. This includes the cost of the casket, which may be up to 50% of the cost of the funeral. It does not include the burial site itself or any of the fees associated with the gravesite. However, this insurance can cover all the expenses of a traditional or other type of service as follows:

- Casket or urn
- · Cremation
- Embalming
- Burial clothing
- Use of the funeral home
- Catering
- Flowers
- Limousine or other transportation

What can you do to make your funeral easier on those you love? Carefully planning your funeral saves money and removes an agonizing experience for your family. You make the decisions yourself based on your own likes and dislikes as well as the costs involved. If you do not preplan, you leave these decisions to those you love when they are already under stress. Sitting in an office in a funeral home and making final decisions that reflect the preferences, costs and sensitivities of each member of your family is a sad and painful experience.

**For those over 50 and in retirement or pre retirement, the insurance to cover funeral expenses can be economically wise and a gift of more than monetary value to your family.**

## *Advantages of prepaid funeral insurance*

- Spares your family from making your funeral plans based on economics alone

- Includes only those options important to you
- Avoids putting an unnecessary financial burden on those closest to you, especially if one member of your family may be responsible for all the costs
- "Locks up" your funeral expenses at today's rate
- Eliminates the awkwardness and difficulty for your family in making financial decisions under stress

**Here are several important concerns to talk about before you buy a prepaid funeral policy from a funeral home:**

- What happens if I move out of state and away from this funeral home?
- What happens if this funeral home goes out of business or changes ownership?
- What specific services are detailed in the contract?
- Can I change the options later?
- Can I get my money back if I change my mind?
- What happens if I die while I am in another state?
- What happens to my payment? What security do I have that the services will be delivered?

Funeral expenses, along with many other services, are continually increasing. However, if you are young, prepaying your funeral expenses may not be your best investment. A temporary or permanent insurance policy from an agent may be a better choice.

On the other hand, for those in retirement, a prepaid funeral could be beneficial to you and your family. Prepaid funerals usually require a full payment or installment payments for two, three, five, even ten years. A separate policy can be added to cover the unpaid amount due if death occurs before the final payment. The added expense may be a trade-off when considering the money saved by "locking in" today's funeral prices.

No matter which option you choose, if you plan and prepay for your own funeral or purchase a life policy to cover costs, your family will be the grateful beneficiary of your forethought and foretalk.

Both specific insurance and prepaid funerals are commonly limited to a maximum payout of between $5,000 and $35,000. Most life policies will not pay out in full until after having been in force for a minimum period, which could be up to 5 years. Prepaid funeral policies with the funeral home as beneficiary, when paid in full, cover expenses as needed.

Remember, neither the cost of a burial plot or mausoleum, opening and closing the grave, a vault, nor a gravestone or marker is included in a prepaid funeral. Prepaid funerals typically cover only the services of the funeral home. (See Chapter Six for information on funeral planning.)

According to a 2007 survey by Funeral and Burial Planners, about ⅓ of funerals in the U.S. involved a form of prepaid funeral or burial insurance.[22] The popularity of prepaid funeral contracts may be because of Medicaid estate planning. As mentioned, a prepaid burial policy is an asset that's permitted under Medicaid rules.

**Insurance protection is an estate-planning tool in a number of ways. Be sure you talk with your insurance professional, financial planner and attorney in reviewing and utilizing the possible benefits of insurance for you and your family.**

# A Totten Trust

Another way to prepay is to self-insure by using a Totten Trust. This little-known bank account can be a simple solution to a complex problem for those with available cash. A Totten Trust is a pay-on-death account at a local bank or credit union. Upon opening the account, a relative, friend, or even a funeral home is chosen as beneficiary. You deposit the amount for your final expenses, and any accrued interest is payable to you. You can close the account any time you want, transfer the balance to a different bank, or change the beneficiary at any time. When you die, the beneficiary collects the account balance and pays for the funeral. This is another example of where legal advice is important.

**Remember to be a wise consumer and compare the features, benefits and costs for the type of insurance you are considering.** You may also want to compare the services and fees of the funeral homes. There are visible differences as well as intangible ones to review.

# Afterthought

In the mid-1800s when life insurance began in the U.S., some religious groups opposed it because they felt insurance made dying a benefit. Some viewed it as gambling. It also sounded too good to be true. But the value to families made life insurance a benefit that workers appreciated and, after a slow start, life insurance and the companies offering coverage became a growing part of the American landscape. Today, for many individuals and families, insurance is one of those difficult purchases to add to their regular expenses. Life or long term care insurance is optional as are policies to cover last expenses. But the value remains for some families. Remember, having insurance places the financial risk somewhere other than on you or your family.

Under the law, buying insurance is elective except when purchasing a home or car. The mortgage lender requires insurance to cover the risk when lending money for your home. If your automobile is not paid for in full, the finance company requires insurance to cover its risk should the car be involved in an accident. Most states require every car that's licensed to be insured. Many people will never collect on either their car or home insurance, but life insurance and prepaid funeral expense are two policies you know will be paid out.

How much financial risk are you willing to assume on behalf of those who depend on you—including the ability to pay your debts and cover expenses for an extended illness that incapacitates you?

This is the kind of question we must be able to answer with clarity. While none of us knows the future, we do acknowledge the need to prepare for the risks ahead. The real question is not only how much risk are you willing to take, but what risk are you willing to place on those you love the most? How can you remove certain financial threats from their future?

What is the right insurance for you? The answer to that question requires foretalk. Do not put this off. Talk to the right people while you can. As I write this a dear friend called and told us her daughter, 48 years old, just passed away after a brief and treatable illness. Because she was young and in good health, there was no foretalk about what could occur, no advance preparation. The expenses and the details were never talked about, multiplying the pain for everyone in the family.

So don't be impressed with those who get rich and pile up fame and fortune. They can't take it with them; fame and fortune all get left behind. Just when they think they've arrived and folks praise them because they've made good, they enter the family burial plot where they'll never see sunshine again.

PSALMS 49:16-17

Before anything happens, talk. Life insurance, long term care insurance and burial insurance should all be considered. Talk with an attorney. Talk with your accountant. As you think about retirement and the possibility of outliving your income, you may find a conversation about an annuity is appropriate. An annuity is one of a limited number of investments that will guarantee a future income stream. Whoever insures your car or your home or provides rental insurance can discuss the insurance policies noted in this chapter.

At one time in this country, insurance was considered a basic need. Insurance salesmen went door-to-door, selling and collecting premiums for life insurance policies. In the decades that followed, the rush to financial success, online trading, speculative brokerage accounts, leveraged real estate and get-rich schemes seemed far more interesting than buying life insurance.

However, the financial turmoil since 2008 has left brokerage accounts depleted, major corporations declaring bankruptcy, and banks everywhere—national, regional, and local—closing their doors. Today insurance policies and annuities have regained some of their luster. Rates being paid on insurance policies and annuities now exceed interest rates available elsewhere.

Perhaps it's time to reassess life insurance as a core holding—not only for its protection, but also for its investment potential.

Go slowly, research your options, talk about insurance with your trusted advisors, and be prepared to navigate your future instead of just waiting, watching, and going wherever the winds may take you.

# PRAYER

*Father God,* we are grateful that we belong to Your forever family. Through Jesus we have been adopted into a full inheritance of blessing now and life eternal ahead. May we be as thoughtful and generous in providing for and protecting our own family. May we be wise and remember that our trust must be only in You. Thank You that the burial plot does not end our family in Christ. AMEN

# Follow-up

| INSURANCE |
|---|
| What kinds of insurance do you currently own? *(List company)* |
| ☐  Automobile: |
| ☐  Homeowners: |
| ☐  Property and casualty: |
| ☐  Renters: |
| ☐  Business interruption: |
| ☐  Health: |
| ☐  Disability: |
| ☐  Other: |
| ☐  Other: |
| ☐  Other: |

### Life Insurance

| | | |
|---|---|---|
| ☐  Personal life insurance company: | | |
| ☐ Temporary *or* ☐ Permanent | | Amount $ |
| ☐  Life insurance company for spouse: | | |
| ☐ Temporary *or* ☐ Permanent | | Amount $ |
| ☐  Group insurance company through employer: | | Amount $ |

### Annuities

| | | |
|---|---|---|
| Do you own an annuity? ☐ Y ☐ N | Company | Amount $ |
| Do you know the amount of income you can expect? ☐ Y ☐ N | | |
| Are you currently receiving income from an annuity? ☐ Y ☐ N | | |
| If so, does that income continue to your spouse? ☐ Y ☐ N | | |

## Burial Policies

| Do you own a burial policy? ☐ Y ☐ N | Company | Amount $ |
|---|---|---|

Do you have a prepaid funeral plan? ☐ Y ☐ N

| Funeral home | Total amount covered $ |
|---|---|

Do you own a prepaid cemetery plot or mausoleum? ☐ Y ☐ N

| Location | Phone |
|---|---|

## Long Term Care Insurance

Do you own long term care insurance? ☐ Y ☐ N

If not, have you reviewed your need for long term care insurance? ☐ Y ☐ N

If yes, what insurance company guarantees your payments?



What is your maximum amount of coverage? $

Have you reviewed your policy and its benefits in the last 3 years? ☐ Y ☐ N

How long will your policy provide coverage?

| Does it have a deductible? ☐ Y ☐ N | Amount $ |
|---|---|

When does the insurance take effect?

## Summary

What other insurance companies do you currently use?









| Who is/are your insurance agent(s)? | Phone |
|---|---|
| | |
| | |
| | |

| |
|---|
| Where are your policies kept? |
| |
| |
| |
| Does your executor or agent for your Durable Powers of Attorney know the location of your policies? ☐ Y ☐ N |
| I have reviewed my insurance program with my agents in the last 3 years. ☐ Y ☐ N |
| I have reviewed beneficiaries in the last 3 years. ☐ Y ☐ N |
| Have there been life changes in the last 3 years (retirement, births or deaths in your family, changes in marital status or changes in relationships)? ☐ Y ☐ N |
| Are these changes reflected in your current insurance policies? ☐ Y ☐ N |
| Do you need to call your insurance professional? ☐ Y ☐ N |
| When will you call? |
| *This is simply the beginning of a complete insurance checklist. As with an attorney, you can talk with an insurance professional at no cost or obligation to you. Ask for referrals to find the right person to work with.* |

*Some people spend more time buying
a car than figuring out where they're going.*

# The SEVENTH *Critical Conversation:*
# Does Our Legacy Demonstrate What Matters Most?
## CHAPTER EIGHT

> Give freely and spontaneously. Don't have a stingy heart. The way you handle matters like this triggers God, your God's blessing in everything you do, all your work and ventures. There are always going to be poor and needy people among you. So I command you: Always be generous, open purse and hands, give to your neighbors in trouble, your poor and hurting neighbors.
>
> DEUTERONOMY 15:10-11

*"I can do things you cannot; you can do things I cannot; together we can do great things."* – *Mother Teresa*

*"The reason God teaches us to give is to save us from our own selfishness and greed. Those are two fatal diseases no amount of money can cure."* – *Robert Morris*

The slums of India were her home; she gave her life ministering to the poorest of the poor. He is called the "Sage of Omaha," one of the world's richest men. What do Mother Teresa and Warren Buffett, two very different people, have in common?

Mother Teresa believed that giving is required of everyone. So does Warren Buffett. She gave her life to her work; he's giving away his entire fortune, his life's work. Though very different in motivation and service, the farthest apart possible in lifestyle, both agree that giving makes life meaningful—for the donor and for a world crying for compassion.

Christians believe all we have comes from one source—our Heavenly Father. Nothing exists that He did not create. He alone is our provision. All of us came into the world with nothing and we will leave in the same way. Our drive, abilities, intellect, ambition, strength are all His gifts to us. The wisest and most successful among us understand and believe that giving back is not only a moral and compassionate act, but there is also a benefit for the donor in ways we cannot begin to imagine.

**Give away your life; you'll find life given back, but not merely given back—given back with bonus and blessing. Giving, not getting, is the way. Generosity begets generosity.** LUKE 6:38

As we think about the final chapter in our lives, it's all the more appropriate to make generosity a central theme in planning our legacy.

## Looking ahead

- **A history of generosity**
- **Andrew Carnegie**
- **Giving and receiving**
- **Little things mean a lot**
- **Increasing your income with a gift**
- **Your children and the children of the world**
- **Legacy giving**

*"The Americans make associations to give entertainment, to found seminaries, to build inns, to construct churches, to diffuse books, to send missionaries to the antipodes; in this manner, they found hospitals, prisons and schools."*

*– Alexis de Tocqueville*

NOTES

# A history of generosity

Giving has a long tradition in the United States.

**Long before the nation was founded, the earliest immigrants planned to create a land of compassion and a culture of caring.**

Even before the Puritans came to America, John Winthrop proposed the new colony be a model of Christian charity. **John Harvard immigrated to the colony of Massachusetts in 1637. He left half of his estate and his entire library, including his collection of theology books, to Cambridge College, a school dedicated to training ministers. Historians estimate the value of the gift at $350, a sizeable amount at the time. His contributions were so significant that Cambridge College was later named Harvard after him.**

Many of the wealthiest families in this country came with nothing, inheriting no position or power, no wealth, no family treasures, no lands or property. They came poor and unassisted. Yet by applying their God-given gifts, they created wealth that transformed their families and the new nation they called their own.

# Andrew Carnegie

*"I resolved to stop accumulating and begin the infinitely more serious and difficult task of wise distribution."*

*– Andrew Carnegie*

Andrew Carnegie was only 13 when his family left Scotland and came to America in 1848. The Carnegies settled in a slum section of Allegheny, Pennsylvania, where Andrew was first employed in a factory. Smart and hard working, he went on to work for a telegraph company and then the Pennsylvania Railroad. He received promotion after promotion, made wise investments, saw his wealth grow, and began to acquire businesses. In his first business, Keystone Bridge Company, he applied new techniques for making steel. Then he expanded his markets, purchasing every phase of the steel-making process. After becoming one of the richest men of his time, he sold everything and began a lifetime of giving away all of his wealth until his death in 1919.

Carnegie's philosophy was simple: "Wealth is not to feed our egos, but to feed the hungry and to help people help themselves." His essay, "The Gospel of Wealth," published in

1889, explained his concept of giving away wealth to benefit society and those sharing least in all its benefits. Among those influenced by Carnegie was John D. Rockefeller. Many of America's greatest fortunes have embraced this tradition of philanthropy.

Andrew Carnegie had noticed, even in his day, that at times the heirs of large fortunes squandered them in "riotous living." Many times families were not emotionally or organizationally equipped to handle large estates and not only lost the wealth but also the vision of those whose work created it in the first place. Setting up foundations to carry out specific goals became the norm following Carnegie's example.

Carnegie believed there were sound reasons for giving away wealth to charitable organizations and foundations. Here is his reasoning:

- **Wealth can be a detriment to your heirs.**
- **The more distant the gift is from the source, the less it is held in esteem.**
- **Organizations and charities have a long life and can adapt to changing social norms and needs.**
- **The needs of charities and missions are usually greater than their resources.**
- **Transparency of charitable organizations makes scrutiny of the stewardship of the organization readily available to every donor.**
- **Starvation, disease, ignorance, discrimination and violation of basic human rights are all social ills that continue to plague our world; but gifts of money and time are lessening the impact of these old enemies of mankind.**
- **Caring for the poor is a fundamental ethical teaching.**[23]

NOTES

Andrew Carnegie left little of his fortune to his children or grandchildren. Kenneth Miller, his grandson, said, "The heritage is richer than any dollar amount he might have left his family."

# Famous American philanthropists

- Andrew Carnegie
- Henry Ford
- Eli Lily
- Milton Hershey
- Robert Wood Johnson
- George Soros
- Warren Buffett
- Bill Gates
- William J. Kellogg
- Oprah Winfrey
- Sam Zell
- T. Boone Pickens
- William Packard
- Peter Lynch
- Paul Newman
- Eli Broad
- J. Paul Getty
- Michael Bloomberg
- Paul Allen
- Ted Turner

Warren Buffett is famous for two things: first, as one of the most talented investors in the world, he amassed one of the biggest fortunes in the U.S.; second, he has an aversion to spending a dime of his $41 billion on anything but what's strictly necessary. That includes declining to provide his kids with fortunes of their own or collecting yachts or racehorses. It may strike some as the supreme paradox that the man who is one of America's greatest misers in life will probably become one of its greatest philanthropists.[24] Not only is he giving away his entire fortune, he is encouraging others to do the same.

**Warren Buffett and Bill Gates made headlines by challenging the 50 wealthiest people in America to give away half their wealth while they are living. As recently as December 2010, more than 55 billionaires signed a "Giving Pledge" to give away the majority of their wealth.** The list includes Mark Zuckerman, the founder of Facebook; Steve Case, the founder of AOL; film director George Lucas; and Larry Ellison, the founder of Oracle. Buffett and Gates were both directly influenced by Andrew Carnegie's book, *The Gospel of Wealth.* The idea of giving away your wealth to benefit those who have little or nothing of their own, to give direct aid to those who are poorest, was as radical in his day as it is in ours.

Speak up for the people who have no voice, for the rights of all the down-and-outers. Speak out for justice! Stand up for the poor and destitute! PROVERBS 31:8-9

# Giving and receiving

Be generous. Give to the poor. Get yourselves a
bank that can't go bankrupt, a bank in heaven
far from bank robbers, safe from embezzlers,
a bank you can bank on. It's obvious, isn't it?
The place where your treasure is, is the place
you will most want to be, and end up being.

LUKE 12:33-34

## *The Treasure Principle*

In Randy Alcorn's book *The Treasure Principle,* he affirms
that "God prospers me not to raise my standard of living,
but to raise my standard of giving."[25]

Every dollar needed to transform the ministry of your
church, your denomination, mission efforts and expressions of compassion for the poor and forgotten is already
available. God has provided it, but His people have not
trusted him enough to give it away. We are all that is stand-
ing between God's great resources and the needs of the
world to have food, clean water and hear the gospel.

**There are very few in our society who lack the
capability to give to others. Giving is a matter of
the heart, not of the pocket.**

God has provided (and promises to provide) more when we
demonstrate our faithfulness. For too many, the focus is not
about being generous but about being careful and cautious.
It's holding back instead of letting go. Our hearts continue
to be grounded in our own backyard. Someone wisely said
that the smallest package in the world is a person wrapped
up in him or herself.

## Compelling reasons to give

- **Giving is the very act of following God's leadership.** God so loved the world that he gave his only Son.
- **Giving is a concrete act of trust.** When we believe that God provides, we give.
- **Giving is living the example of Jesus.** He gave up everything as God's son to live as a man. He poured out his life on the cross.
- **Giving frees us from the cancer of materialism—the drive to accumulate stuff.** We have trashed our world and our lives with discardable, disposable, destructive "stuff" that has filled our planet, our homes and our days with poor substitutes for the presence of God.
- **Giving makes space for God to fill.** A closed hand can't hold anything new until it lets go of whatever it is clutching. "Stuff" demands attention, time and thought, just to be taken care of.

- **Giving means multiplication, not subtraction.** A little boy's lunch was freely given to a disciple who brought it to Jesus. It was not taken away but multiplied so that basketfuls of loaves and fish fed more than 5,000 people and full baskets still remained.
- **Giving is the only way to meet the needs of a world filled with ignorance, starvation and death.** Those who have claimed much of the world's resources must share with those who have little. A hand up is not a handout. Who else should help if not you?
- **Giving is an acknowledgment of an act of grace.** Giving to those who can give nothing in return is recognition of the grace we ourselves have received.

*"He said: Freely, freely, you have received;*
*Freely, freely give; Go in My name,*
*and because you believe*
*Others will know that I live."*[26]

Both our time and our money are resources that belong to Him. Christian philanthropy ought to have champions who stand up and declare they are following God's leadership by the gifts they give to others. Recall what Jesus said about letting your light shine.

Here's another way to put it: You're here to be light, bringing out the God-colors in the world. God is not a secret to be kept. We're going public with this, as public as a city on a hill. If I make you light-bearers, you don't think I'm going to hide you under a bucket, do you? I'm putting you on a light stand. Now that I've put you there on a hilltop, on a light stand—

shine! Keep open house; be generous with your lives. By opening up to others, you'll prompt people to open up with God, this generous Father in heaven. MATTHEW 5:14-16

# Little things mean a lot

While the gifts of the wealthy make headlines, it's the combined gifts of smaller amounts that consistently support the majority of charities and non-profit organizations.

## Cash gifts

Cash gifts are a major source of funding for local and global charities. Even the smallest donations become meaningful contributions, carrying with them the gifts of compassion and love from the donor. Sometimes our smallest gifts can have the greatest meaning. No story illustrates this better than this example from Jesus.

Just then he looked up and saw the rich people dropping offerings in the collection plate. Then he saw a poor widow put in two pennies. He said, "The plain truth is that this widow has given by far the largest offering today. All these others made offerings that they'll never miss; she gave extravagantly what she couldn't afford—she gave her all!" LUKE 21:1-4

I worked my way through college with some help from scholarships and loans. However, the most meaningful assistance came from the generosity of others. Milton Neal, Gifford Blyton and Russ Mobley were just a few who provided support. But no letters were more appreciated

than those from my grandmother—always with a $5 gift enclosed.

Every charity—whether helping the needy, providing disaster relief, medical research, and educational funds, supporting our troops, or sustaining your church or house of worship—depends on your cash gifts of any size.

# Appreciated assets

Most Americans keep the majority of their assets in illiquid investments such as their home, investment real estate, pensions, annuity contacts, and/or retirement accounts. Cash represents the smallest portion of what we possess. Yet when it comes to giving, our gifts most often come from our cash, not our assets that have higher monetary value. Why not give a much more meaningful gift (in size and potential impact) by tapping into your larger pool of assets?

**The most tax-efficient gifts are those you give on which taxes would have had to be paid.** This includes gifts from an IRA and long-term capital gains from property that has significant appreciation. At this writing, anyone who is at least 70½ years old can make a gift from a retirement account without paying income taxes on its distribution.

You can also give real estate and/or appreciated securities. Your donation reflects their appreciated value without your paying capital gains taxes. This is smart giving. It not only increases what you can give, but can be a significant gift to a number of ministries.

# Beneficiary designations

**Designating your church or other charity as a beneficiary of a life insurance policy or making it the beneficiary of all or a portion of your retirement account can have an impact far beyond a simple cash gift.** Reviewing life insurance policies and the beneficiaries of your will or retirement accounts is wise. Many times, a much-needed review of a will written long ago not only solves potential family problems, but can also significantly benefit charities of importance to you.

Kathy's uncle had written his will over 25 years ago while in his late 60s. Fifty percent of his assets were to go to Kathy's parents and the remainder was to be equally divided among Kathy and her nine cousins. Many things had changed in the last 20 years, including the deaths of both of Kathy's parents. The property noted in his will had appreciated 10 times over.

Kathy told me, "I'm talking with my uncle now to be sure the will as written is what he currently wants. The half going to my parents would now come to me. Then the ten cousins, including me, would divide the other half. It would create a huge family problem. No one knew what my uncle had planned until he asked me to review his will." (Kathy is an attorney.) "One look and I knew we'd all be arguing and fighting if we didn't get this resolved. He wants to treat us all equally, but unless his will is updated that won't happen. We could also have a serious estate tax problem. He needs a new will. He now wants to make a number of charitable gifts, including a gift to his church. But he needs to do it now."

# Increasing your income with a gift

You can give in ways that can demonstrate your support for your chosen charities and, at the same time, benefit you now.

**One "life income" strategy is a Charitable Gift Annuity. It allows you to set up a future gift to a charity as well as receive a fixed income stream you cannot outlive.** The income created from this type of gift may be greater than the income found anywhere else. It is determined by your age. The older you are, the greater the income paid to you.

The Charitable Gift Annuity is especially appealing in a low-interest-rate environment. The income can be paid to you alone or you and another person.

In addition to increasing income from low-yielding assets, a Charitable Gift Annuity can reduce or eliminate capital gains as well as estate and/or gift taxes. Donors receive a charitable income tax deduction equal to the present

NOTES

value of the future gift to the charity. Gift Annuity payment rates can begin at 5% and can go as high as 9.5% for a donor 90 years old or older.

> ## *Additional facts to consider*
>
> - The income received is partially tax-free as a return of principal.
> - The gift is irrevocable. Your heirs cannot change the terms.
> - The amount remaining at your death may be more or less than the amount given, depending on the amount of the annuity payments to you.
> - The principal is not guaranteed and will be affected over time by investment gains or losses.

Rather than making a large one-time gift, laddering Charitable Gift Annuities can be a smart strategy if interest rates are projected to rise. Laddering simply means giving multiple smaller gifts as rates rise. There is no limit to the number of charitable gift trusts you may establish.

## Giving income but retaining the principal

A **Charitable Lead Trust** is a way to give to a charity and allow the donor to maintain control of the gift. This means it's possible to make a charitable gift using funds that will eventually be returned to you or your loved ones.

**With a Charitable Lead Trust the income goes to the charity and the remainder returns to the donor, donor's beneficiaries, or heirs after a stated period.** In effect, this is the reverse of a Charitable Remainder Annuity Trust. There are numerous types of trusts, many more than those mentioned here.

The tax benefit to the donor is one of the reasons trusts are valuable. Indeed, the largest foundations in the world are based on the creation of a trust.

But don't think charitable trusts are only for the extremely wealthy. **A charitable trust can be funded with smaller amounts, and the charity may provide legal guidance at no cost to the donor.**

## Giving from accumulated assets

Here is a wide variety of ways to give to the charities closest to your heart:
- Tithe 10% of your assets at death to your charity in your will.
- Make the church or charity a 10% (or more) beneficiary of your retirement account or insurance policy.

- Donate your car, boat, or RV—either now or in your will.
- Instruct the bank to pay out your savings or checking account to your designated beneficiary at your death. Any amount of the balance can go to your charity by signing a simple form at your bank.

# The probate process

The purpose of probate is to determine and distribute your assets and property according your will and state laws. You have probably heard that you should avoid going through the probate system. This process is not necessarily as difficult as we are led to believe and is not always a problem. However, it can tie up property for months and may be costly if it is not thought through.

**Much of the effort to wrap up a person's affairs— like paying hospital and funeral bills and other creditors—is necessary even if probate court is avoided entirely.** The probate process often goes smoothly and, when it doesn't, it's often because someone has challenged the will. Any challenges will delay the process and run up attorneys' fees. That is why you need a well-drafted will.

Since attorneys' fees for probate can vary widely and may be based on estate assets, it makes sense to lower the value of the estate. It will reduce both the tax bill and attorney's fees.

## How to reduce the size of your estate

- It is most common to have joint ownership of property. This means only 50% of the property value is in the estate.

- Payable-on-death bank accounts or transfer-on-death securities accounts will move those assets from your estate to your beneficiary without probate.
- At this writing, children may be given up to $13,000 a year from each parent without incurring gift taxes. Over the years, a substantial amount can be given away.
- Charitable transfers at death allow an unlimited removal of assets from an estate while keeping them for your use during your lifetime.

Comprehensive strategies to deal with probate are available. If your estate exceeds $5 million, be sure to discuss the options with a tax attorney and/or a certified public accountant for more complete information.

# Your children and the children of the world

When you harvest your land, don't harvest right up to the edges of your field or gather the gleanings from the harvest. Don't strip your vineyard bare or go back and pick up the fallen grapes. Leave them for the poor and the foreigner.

I am God, your God.
LEVITICUS 19:9-10

In the list of resources, you will find a book called *The Mom's Guide to Wills and Estate Planning* by Lisa Hanks. The title of Chapter 3 always makes me laugh: "Leave Money to Your Kids? Are You Nuts?"

In a *Fortune* magazine article "Should You Leave it All to the Children?"[27] the author quotes a number of wealthy families and advisers to the wealthy who cite historical and contemporary examples of the damage that inheriting wealth can do to families. One person he interviewed was Warren Buffett, who has publicly declared he isn't leaving his fortune to his children. Buffett is quoted as saying that he believes setting up his heirs with "a lifetime supply of food stamps just because they came out of the right womb" can be "harmful" for children and is "an antisocial act." To him the perfect amount to leave children is "enough money so that they would feel they could do anything, but not so much that they could do nothing."

**Those with more modest means than Buffett typically plan to leave the bulk of their assets to their children. However, in recent years, more families are also remembering the children of the world by making charities a component of their estate planning.** Charities such as World Vision and Feed the Children, UNICEF, and numerous others can provide food and medical care for children around the world for just a few dollars. These organizations not only give immediate assistance, but also dig wells for clean water and provide the education, seed and equipment for tilling gardens. They build schools and other training centers to help the poor find their way out of seemingly hopeless situations.

# Legacy giving

When you include your church or other charities in your will, you are following Biblical principles and the example of some of the wealthiest and wisest people in America. **This is one of the easiest, most meaningful and most forgotten ways to give. Simply adding your church, charitable foundation or another meaningful charity as one of the beneficiaries of your estate is a gift that can outlive your life and provide long-term support where it is sorely needed.** Tithing your accumulated assets through a bequest is one more way to follow the Biblical mandate and the teachings of Jesus.

Making meaningful current gifts of stocks, real estate or cash can make a difference to the organization you support. It also makes a statement about your values and character. Choosing to include your church or a ministry in your will creates a long-term asset for the ministry that makes its future more secure.

Remember, this may need to be a conversation with your heirs. Help them understand that your desire to bless others comes from the same God who provided for you to bless them. This may remove untimely surprises and be an important topic for foretalk.

NOTES

*"A wise woman who was traveling in the mountains found a precious stone in a stream. The next day she met another traveler who was hungry, and the wise woman opened her bag to share her food. The hungry traveler saw the precious stone and asked the woman to give it to him. She did so without hesitation. The traveler left, rejoicing in his good fortune. He knew the stone was worth enough to give him security for a lifetime. But a few days later he came back to return the stone to the wise woman. 'I've been thinking,' he said. 'I know how valuable the stone is, but I give it back in the hope that you can give me something even more precious. Give me what you have within you that enabled you to give me the stone.'"*

*– Author Unknown*

**Generosity is a matter of the heart.** It is being fearless about the future. A lifestyle of generosity is a multiplied blessing to both donor and recipients.

Perhaps there is no better way to write the final chapter of your life than by an act of compassion that provides for the needs of those beyond your family circle.

Hallelujah! I give thanks to God with everything I've got— wherever good people gather, and in the congregation. God's works are so great, worth a lifetime of study—endless enjoyment! Splendor and beauty mark his craft; His generosity never gives out. His miracles are his memorial— This God of grace, this God of love. He gave food to those who fear Him; He remembered to keep his ancient promise. He proved to his people that He could do what He said: Hand them the nations on a platter—a gift! He manufactures truth and justice; all His products are guaranteed to last—Never out-of-date, never obsolete, rustproof. All that he makes and does is honest and true: He paid the ransom for his people, He ordered His covenant kept forever. He's so personal and holy, worthy of our respect. The good life begins in the fear of God—Do that and you'll know the blessing of God. His hallelujah lasts forever! PSALMS 111:1-10

# Afterthought

Recently a reality television show called "Hoarders" allowed us to see the cluttered homes and the chaotic lives of those who could not bear to part with anything. The reality is that some have homes full of "stuff," but have very empty lives. **When we honestly ask ourselves who in our lives has meant the most to us, it is not those who have the most. More often it is those who have given when the need was the greatest. Those who gave stand head and shoulders above those who had the most.**

Current laws in our country support charitable giving by providing tax deductions based on our gifts. But if all the laws providing tax deductions were to disappear tomorrow, it would make no difference to a generous heart. There are higher-level laws that compel us to be faithful in our giving.

There are those in your family, your neighborhood, your church and community who are in need right now—financial need, need for recognition, involvement, or—caring that communicates a feeling of significance. Demonstrate your generosity.

Today you can choose to bless and enrich lives all around you. Long after you are gone, your generosity may be remembered in the lives of others. Practice your generosity today. Make a LASTing impression with a testimony of God's blessing to you and your family by blessing others.

Know your options. Talk with a tax attorney as well as a board member or foundation member of your church or other charity. There is a wealth of information that is yours for the asking. Review your options. Consider making a major gift, creating a charitable trust, including your church or charitable organization as the beneficiary of 10% or more of your estate, retirement account, or other assets. You may find legal and personal help just by asking.

Generosity is contagious. Don't be surprised at the pleasure that comes from being generous. The gift you make and the example you set could be the beginning of an ongoing flow of gifts that change the future for those who least expect your kindness.

> **I'm telling the solemn truth:** Whenever you did one of these things to someone overlooked or ignored, that was me—you did it to me.
>
> MATTHEW 25:40

# PRAYER

*Dear Heavenly Father,* there is no end of Your generosity toward us. We are continually amazed at the blessings that are so freely given—far beyond anything we deserve. You have poured out Your love in creation and given it a name in Jesus. We have experienced the generosity of Your Son in giving us His all, even His life and then the reality of life eternal in His resurrection. May we end our selfish and soulless love of things and follow the witness and will of Your only Son. May we be known as the most generous of people by our willingness to give to others with the same generosity we have received. Teach us to live with an open hand and open heart and a willingness to bless others just as we have been blessed by You. AMEN

# Follow-up

| YOUR PLANNING GUIDE TO GENEROSITY | | |
|---|---|---|
| I have recognized God's provision in my life and will be faithful and generous to the work of his kingdom by giving: | | |
| ☐ From my cash assets | | |
| ☐ From my accumulated assets | | |
| ☐ I have made God's work a beneficiary in my will. | | |
| Churches or other faith-based organizations to be remembered in your gifts: | | |
| *Name* | *Type of gift* | *% or Amount* |
| | | |
| | | |

## Public charities *(e.g., Red Cross, Goodwill Industries, United Way)*:

| Name | Type of gift | % or Amount |
|------|--------------|-------------|
|  |  |  |
|  |  |  |
|  |  |  |
|  |  |  |
|  |  |  |
|  |  |  |
|  |  |  |

## Global relief organizations *(e.g., UNICEF, OXFAM, World Vision, Feed the Children)*:

| Name | Type of gift | % or Amount |
|------|--------------|-------------|
|  |  |  |
|  |  |  |
|  |  |  |

## Charitable beneficiary designations in my will/insurance/retirement accounts:

| Description | Amount |
|-------------|--------|
|  |  |
|  |  |
|  |  |
|  |  |

*Contacts/Calls to make regarding changes to my beneficiaries:*

| | | |
|---|---|---|
| | | |
| | | |
| | | |

**Appreciated assets to be given:**

| Recipient | Description | Amount |
|---|---|---|
| **STOCKS, MUTUAL FUNDS** | | |
| | | |
| | | |
| | | |
| **REAL ESTATE** | | |
| | | |
| | | |
| | | |

**Personal property to be given:**

| Recipient | Description | Amount |
|---|---|---|
| **AUTOMOBILE(S) AND OTHER TRANSPORTATION, RECREATIONAL VEHICLES, BOATS** | | |
| 1 | | |
| 2 | | |
| 3 | | |
| **ITEMS OF PERSONAL PROPERTY** | | |
| Item A: | | |
| | | |
| Item B: | | |
| | | |

| Item C: |
| --- |
| |
| Item D: |
| |
| Item E: |
| |
| Item F: |
| |
| Item G: |
| |
| Item H |
| |

**GIVING GIFTS NOW INSTEAD OF INCLUDING THEM IN YOUR ESTATE WILL BE SIMPLER AND ALLOW YOU TO SEE THE BENEFITS OF YOUR GENEROSITY.**

| Item A: |
| --- |
| *To whom?* |
| Item B: |
| *To whom?* |
| Item C: |
| *To whom?* |
| Item D: |
| *To whom?* |
| Item E: |
| *To whom?* |

# Living In
# The Season of Now

## CHAPTER NINE

God gives out Wisdom free, is plainspoken in Knowledge
and Understanding. He's a rich mine of Common Sense for those
who live well, a personal bodyguard to the candid and sincere.
He keeps his eye on all who live honestly, and pays special attention
to his loyally committed ones. So now you can pick out what's true
and fair, find all the good trails! Lady Wisdom will be your close
friend, and Brother Knowledge your pleasant companion.
Good Sense will scout ahead for danger, Insight will keep
an eye out for you. They'll keep you from making wrong turns,
or following the bad directions of those who are lost
themselves and can't tell a trail from a tumbleweed.

PROVERBS 2:6-13

*"If life were fair, Elvis would be alive and
the impersonators would be dead."*

*– Johnny Carson*

*"The majority of human beings behave as though death
were no more than an unfounded rumor."*

*– Aldus Huxley*

We've always been told we have only one opportunity to make a first impression. The truth is, over time, you can change a first impression. But you will never be able to change a last impression. **After your death the memories left**

**behind cannot be altered.** *ForeTalk* is about leaving positive and LASTing impressions. **No one knows what day will be the day of last impressions.**

*"Almost everything—all external expectations, all pride, all fear of embarrassment or failure— these things fall away in the face of death, leaving only what is truly important...There is no reason not to follow your heart."*
*– Steve Jobs, Stanford Commencement, 2005*

January 15, 2009, US Air Flight 1549 was on its way to Charlotte, North Carolina, when, two minutes after takeoff, a flock of Canada geese flew into the aircraft causing both engines to fail. The passengers braced for impact. As the plane fell from the sky, the freezing waters of the Hudson came into view and Flight 1549 hit the water at 150 mph. Dave Sanderson, a businessman on the plane, said in a television interview, "When you think you're going to die, you start thinking about your life…your family, little league baseball, things like in a movie."[28] All 156 passengers survived the crash in the 36° water, but their lives were changed forever.

## When the clock is that loud

**When you become personally acquainted with death, you place a higher value on life, gain a heightened clarity about the value of time and a renewed focus on using it well.** James Patterson, a best-selling author, described his experience in a recent interview.[29]

*"Thirty years ago, I was in an idyllic relationship with a wonderful woman. One day we were in the post office when she had a seizure. Jane had a brain tumor, and for the next two and a half years she was dying. But I'd always say, 'Isn't it lucky that you didn't die in the post office, and we are still here today?'* **We are all dying but life becomes so clear when the clock is that loud.** *I am grateful to live with that awareness."*

Arch Oboler (1907-1987), American playwright, screenwriter, novelist, producer and director, used this theme for a radio drama, "The Mirage." It was first performed on his NBC radio series, "Arch Oboler Playhouse," popular in the golden age of radio and, today, a favorite on satellite radio.

Oboler tells the story of a couple walking into the night who, through mysterious circumstances, believed their lives were soon coming to an end and made drastic changes in their plans. **The drama ended with a poignant closing line: "Why did it take death for us to learn how to live?"**[30]

**As my brother came face to face with death and heard "the loud ticking of the clock," he recalled things he wished he had done to change his life, the things he'd meant to do but kept putting off until "the right time."** Unlike the characters in the radio play, it was too late. He longed for just a little more time but had lost his opportunity. May you never have similar unresolved regrets.

## Looking ahead

- **7 lessons from a hospital bed**
- **First things first**
- **Missing what's important**
- **Living in the season of now**

# 7 lessons from a hospital bed

After my brother's hospitalization for lung cancer, we had 41 days to talk before he passed away. With each passing day our conversations took on more urgency. Here are 7 lessons I learned from Ron:

### 1 Make every day count.
"I simply can't believe that I'm dying—I'm only 61. There are still so many things I wanted to do. I never thought I was running out of time. I can barely lift my head to get a drink of water. I have wasted so much time."

### 2 Get your priorities in order.
"I was always a hard worker; I was known for that. I just wish I'd worked as hard on my relationships. The only thing that matters now is all of you around me in this hospital room. I thought I was all right—doing what I had to do. But truth is, I messed up."

### 3 Don't wait to do the right thing.

"Why did I wait to get things right with Betty?" (He'd re-established a loving relationship with Betty, his estranged wife, in the previous six months.) "I wanted to spend time with her and the kids but I was afraid. I don't know what I was afraid of—I needed them and they needed me. I wasted time. I knew what to do—just didn't do it."

### 4 Don't neglect the important people in your life.

"My kids came all the way from Tennessee and Mississippi just to be with me. Now I realize just how important we are to each other. I have a great family and, right now, they are the reason I want to get out of here."

### 5 Stop the habits you know are killing you.

"I didn't think I could get by without my cigarettes, and I guess I didn't think my life mattered much. Now my life is the only thing that matters and cigarette smoking took it away. I knew my coughing was bad but not that bad. How could I have done this (to myself)?"

### 6 Your faith matters. Grow it; you will need it.

"I don't have anything right now—nothing but time to think. I know God is with me and cares about me. But I should have given time to Him to live like I knew I should. This is a scary place, Brother."

### 7 Your life is coming to an end faster than you think.

"I didn't know how many things I wanted to do until I realized I couldn't do anything anymore. I always thought I had the time; I'd get around to it. There was always tomorrow. Not any more."

As Christmas came and went, his body became less and less able to tolerate treatment. It was apparent that radiation

NOTES

and chemo were no longer helpful. The new year began and Ron was aware there would be no more New Years for him to celebrate. He passed away just a few days after moving to hospice.

**Having time to talk about important things is a gift—one that's frequently left unopened. Many of us tend to see "busyness" as a virtue and the clock becomes the master of our lives. Somehow we lose our sense of worth when work and activity decline.** It's no accident that the logo for *ForeTalk* has a clock at its center.

It seems there have never been more things to occupy our lives. Smart phones are not only our telephones but our computers and cameras, storing our memories as well as our calendars! And we need calendars. Our days are filled with planning and shopping; entertaining; meetings; transporting children; visiting doctors and dentists;

going to lunch or dinner; maintaining our car(s) and our house(s); cleaning and cooking; watching television and reading books, newspapers or magazines; checking our emails; responding to/reviewing/deleting electronic newsletters, sales, coupons, and unsolicited spam. It isn't any wonder that people say, "I simply don't have time."

**What if you knew you really didn't have time? Would you change your schedule?**

# First things first

"First things first" is wonderful advice, but it's not the way most of us live our lives. As Steven Covey explains, "First things are those things you, personally, find of most worth. If you put first things first, you are organizing and managing time and events according to the personal priorities you established."[31]

*"When we get too caught up in the busyness of the world we lose connection with one another—and ourselves."*
*– Jack Kornfield*

*"Much of the stress that people feel doesn't come from having too much to do. It comes from not finishing what they started."*
*– David Allen*

Having too few hours generally isn't the problem; the problem is establishing priorities. What are your real priorities? Are you letting meaningless activities or inactivity crowd out what you ought to be doing? **Are there things you need to end in order to get to the important things you want to accomplish?**

In his book *Necessary Endings*[32] Dr. Henry Cloud gives a list of reasons why we avoid endings in our lives. Here are just a few:

- We fear confrontation.
- We are afraid of hurting someone.
- We are afraid of letting go and the sadness associated with an ending.
- We are afraid of the unknown.
- We do not know the right words to use.
- We have had too many painful endings in our personal history, so we avoid another one.

Endings are just one aspect of getting to our priorities. At times we lose track of what is important because of all the clutter we have allowed to distract us. Creating your own endings allows you to regain control of your life and focus on what's really significant.

NOTES

# Missing what's important

Here's an example: Richard and Carrie have just finished renovating the interior of their home. It took several weeks to complete at considerable cost. However, while the house has never looked better, the family is falling apart. Richard's work keeps him away from home most of the week and, because Carrie receives little attention from Rick, she has little to give back. They have limited communication and no intimacy. After years of living in this troubled relationship, they're discussing divorce. Sadly, their two school-aged children are living in a beautiful house but are watching their home disintegrate.

If they had stopped to think which is more important, keeping the family emotionally secure or choosing any other worthy activity, the family would have come first. **The problem is that we seldom stop to think. The immediate replaces the important.** What we usually discover is when "this," whatever it is, is over, there is another "this" to take its place. As a result, we let life happen. Like a painting out of the frame, something is missing and the edges begin to fray; the images we saw of our future lose the clarity and the influence they once had.

**But what if we were more aware of the passing of time, the loud ticking of the clock and the end of our days? Would our lives better reflect our priorities? Would we end the distractions and focus on where we wanted to be all along?**

## What if we numbered our days?

The lyrics of the Tim McGraw hit song, "Live Like You Were Dyin'," describes what life could be if we behaved as if we really knew our time was limited.

Perhaps the most significant part of this popular song is the line repeated in the chorus, "someday I hope you get the chance to live like you're dying.[33]"

We all have that opportunity. If we will simply respond to the biblical teaching that we are to, "number our days", and by doing so, "apply our hearts to wisdom" , the value of knowing the end of life is coming will be ours.

This song's popularity tells us McGraw's message has meaning for many.

Over the years, as this book was being written, nearly everyone I have met has a story to tell about a recent death in their family or among their acquaintances. Their stories are most often about the tragic consequences resulting from someone very dear and near to them not being prepared when death interrupted.

Life would be so much simpler if we all knew in which season of life we are living and what the next season would bring. However, that knowledge is denied us all. We do know one thing for sure; our existence here will end. How we prepare will impact everyone we know and especially those who love us most. **Life goes on even when your life doesn't.**

Living in the season of now is the time for these critical conversations. Do not put off living fully in the present and that means preparing and creating the kind of future we want our family and loved ones to enjoy, especially when we are no longer here to share those moments with them.

*"One of the most tragic things I know about human nature is that all of us tend to put off living.*

*We are all dreaming of some magical rose garden over the horizon— instead of enjoying the roses blooming outside our windows today."*
*– Dale Carnegie*

# Do not put off living

**Making the most of your days may not mean what you think it does.**

Our culture spends a lot of time working to be more productive. We are constantly looking for ways to discover more timesaving technology. "Making the most of our time" has become a maddening obsession. We are a multitasking, activity-focused, "git'er-done" society who look down on leisure and praise those who "burn out" rather than "rust out." At the same time we are stressed out, worn out, tired out, and striking out with our families and our own bodies. The result is seen every day in the news:

* Depression
* Sleep disorders
* Anxiety
* High blood pressure
* Heart disease
* Drug addition
* Spouse and children abuse

**Perhaps "making the most of our time" ought to mean more time spent with those we love, doing what we love.** Dr. Jim Loehr says it this way: "The richest, happiest, and most productive lives are characterized by the ability to fully engage in the challenge at hand, but also to disengage periodically and seek renewal."[34]

# Living in the season of now

**1 Take one day this month and ask yourself, "What is really important to me?"**

This doesn't require spending money or traveling. Simply turn off your computer, TV, radio, and cell phone and take a walk–alone. Visit a nearby park and have a frank talk with yourself and with God. If you knew your life were coming to an end, perhaps sooner than planned, perhaps this month, this year, or today would be very important to you. Live like you were dying.

**2 Let "no" become part of your vocabulary.**

You cannot do everything you are capable of doing if you do everything you are asked to do. **No one else knows your personal dreams like you do. No one will be as impacted as you if you fail to make them happen.** Accept only those invitations that are relevant to your dreams, your life and your family. "No" can be a positive response. It is not only acceptable but also desirable to say, "I'm sorry, but my calendar is already full." There are necessary endings. Your priorities matter. Live like you were dying.

**3 View time as a depleting resource.**
There is no endless supply of time no

matter your age or station in life. Have you ever heard someone say you could buy time? That's wrong. You may be able to delay an event but you cannot buy time. Once an hour is spent, it's gone forever. Only today exists and how we use it matters. Today is the perfect day to use your time well. Live like you were dying.

## 4 Clear out the dark shadows.

If you need to ask forgiveness, now is the time. If you need to pay a debt or give a gift, now is the time. If destructive habits still rule your life, now is the time to end them. If you need to repent, do it now. If you own things that would embarrass you if a member of your family found them after your death, get rid of them now. **In fact, think of all you're holding on to that you should let go of. Do it now.** Necessary endings. Live like you were dying.

## 5 Start living your priorities and end procrastination.

If you are like most, you are busy! There are things you are doing because you believe you need to do them right now. When they are taken care of, then you will do the things that are most important to you. That's a trap from which there is little or no escape. Work will always be there, demands will always be there; children won't, spouses may not, families won't, time won't be there either. **Do your required work, but use your time as if it was the most precious thing in your life. It is.**

## 6 Remember: To everything there is a season.

Attending a meeting, writing a report or sitting in a conference may be important, but taking time for the important people or goals in your life is essential. Playing

NOTES

horseshoes or golf with friends, reading to your child, talking with your family, taking a drive or a trip to visit friends, taking a walk or riding your bike—all these perceived time-wasters—may be your best use of time for a particular day. **There is a season for everything, a time for everything. Just put your priorities in order.** Write them down. Let your seasons of life be enriched with wisdom in what you choose to do. Live like you were dying.

Is there something you want to do before you die—visit Paris, go on a mission trip to Africa, write your book, paint landscapes, talk about your faith with someone important to you, share a sporting or entertainment event? What's on your "bucket list"[35] that you haven't accomplished yet? Write it down and find a way to get it moving. Put a completion date on it. Start planning now. Live like you were dying.

*"Somebody should tell us, right at the start of our lives, that we are dying. Then we might live life to the limit, every minute of every day. Do it! I say. Whatever you want to do, do it now! There are only so many tomorrows."*
*– Pope Paul VI*

**Last impressions are the most important of all because they last longest and are most treasured.** The ones you love the most, the friends you care about and causes you believe in can be blessed by your thoughtful last impressions. Or not. You may be making your last impression right now. Live like you were dying.

Do you want your loved ones to remember that you were hard to live with, tough on others, angry, mean-spirited? Or that you always had a smile and a ready laugh, a generous heart and spirit, helped those in need, a person who followed God's leading? **You are creating lasting impressions every day of your life. Live them carefully. Your legacy, including memories and impressions, is being created now.** Painful memories can fade if we replace them with beautiful memories… make them last.

**J. M. Barrie, author of *Peter Pan*, said, "God gives us memory so that we may have roses in December."** Roses in December—what a beautiful thought.

**You have the opportunity to create your last impression starting today.** Make it your very best. Before significant end-of-life issues arrive, talk about them. Don't avoid conversation simply because you believe it will be painful. The worst pain for your loved ones comes when you are no longer there to share your thoughts, your love, your concern.

**Roses in December are a result of meaningful foretalk.** You took the first step toward significant conversation when you read this book. **It is our prayer that _ForeTalk_ will inspire you to plant the seeds that will result in roses in December—that, in this season of your life, you will be conscious of the passing of time and live every day to the fullest—and that you'll take time to prepare your family for a future when your memories will be as meaningful as roses that bloom in December.**

# Afterthought

One way to recall new ideas you have discovered as you read this book is to review it from back to front. This may not make sense to you right now, but try it. I think you will find it really works. You'll get a fresh view of the content and the logic of the outline. Then talk to the important people in your life. Talk to your trusted advisors. Check off your accomplishments in your *ForeTalk* planning checklist. Get the documents prepared, the will written or reviewed, the funeral and all arrangements taken care of. Set a deadline and keep it. Before any serious event takes place in your life, talk about it.

*ForeTalk* ends just as it began with a paraphrase of the prayer of the Psalmist:

**Now teach us to remember our days are numbered so we may be wise in how we spend them.** PSALMS 92:12

## Your *ForeTalk* Checklist

Have you had the seven critical conversations you need and want to have?

## My *ForeTalk* planning checklist:

- [ ] My *letter of gratitude* has been written.
- [ ] My *will* is completed and updated.
- [ ] My *Durable Power of Attorney for Finances* is completed.
- [ ] My *Durable Power of Attorney for Health Care* is completed.
- [ ] My *Living Will* is completed.
- [ ] My *insurance* has been reviewed.
- [ ] I have discussed and described my *funeral / memorial* in writing.
- [ ] My *gifts* have been designated to ministry and charities.
- [ ] My family has reviewed and discussed my *wishes*.
- [ ] My *priorities* are in place and I am living them now to the best of my ability.
- [ ] I am content and ready to enjoy all my coming days because these concerns are all behind me.
- [ ] I am secure in my *plans* and know that foretalk is better than hindsight.

No one knows what lies ahead. Being content and prepared for all your tomorrows isn't difficult, it just requires commitment, some forethought, and a lot of foretalk. **Remember, your last impression is important to those you love.**

**These seven critical conversations are designed so that you can claim as your own this closing thought which Paul sent to the brothers and sisters in the church at Philippi.**

## A CLOSING THOUGHT

I'm glad in God, far happier than you would ever guess—happy that you're again showing such strong concern for me... Actually, I don't have a sense of needing anything personally. I've learned by now to be quite content whatever my circumstances. I'm just as happy with little as with much, with much as with little. I've found the recipe for being happy whether full or hungry, hands full or hands empty. Whatever I have, wherever I am, I can make it through anything in the One who makes me who I am. PHILIPPIANS 4:10-13

# APPENDIX

## Key document checklist and location

*(Once you have completed each document, please check the box and fill in the information below.)*

☐ **PERSONAL PROPERTY INVENTORY**
Date: _____
Location: _____

☐ **LETTER OF GRATITUDE**
Date: _____
Location: _____

☐ **LAST WILL AND TESTAMENT**
Date: _____
Location: _____

☐ **DURABLE POWER OF ATTORNEY FOR HEALTH CARE**
Date: _____
Location: _____

☐ **DURABLE POWER OF ATTORNEY FOR FINANCES**
Date: _____
Location: _____

☐ **LIVING WILL**
Date: _____
Location: _____

☐ **FUNERAL OR MEMORIAL PLAN**
Date: _____
Location: _____

☐ **SAFE DEPOSIT BOX**
Location of key: _____

☐ **USERNAMES & PASSWORDS**
U/N _____ PW _____ for _____
U/N _____ PW _____ for _____
U/N _____ PW _____ for _____
U/N _____ PW _____ for _____
U/N _____ PW _____ for _____

# RESOURCES

**INTERNET –** There are hundreds of valuable resources on the Internet. These are just a few of those cited and reviewed in *ForeTalk*:

- **www.aarp.org/magazine**
  American Association of Retired Persons Magazine

- **www.agingwithdignitiy.org**
  "Five Wishes" Living Will document.

- **www.alz.org**
  Alzheimer's Association

- **www.anatomicgift.com**
  The Anatomy Gifts Registry For Organ Donors

- **www.cancer.org**
  American Cancer Society

- **www.assistedlivinginfo.com**
  Guide for selecting an assisted living facility

- **www.caringinfo.org**
  National Hospice and Palliative Care Organization

- **www.cms.hhs.gov**
  Medicare and Medicaid help and answers

- **www.eldercare.gov**
  Eldercare locator

- **www.elderlawanswers.com**
  Full information on elder law attorneys

- **www.findlaw.com**
  Thompson Reuters site with information on current legal issues

- **www.longtermcare.gov**
  Complete guide to LTC

- **www.mayoclinic.com**
  Health and wellness information

- **www.mayoclinic.com/health/ organ-donation/FL00077**
  Organ donation explained

- **www.medicare.com**
  Official site with complete information

- **www.militaryconnections. com/burial_honors.cfm**
  Veteran funeral benefits

- **www.nolo.com**
  The nation's oldest provider of legal information for consumers

- **www.iaod.org**
  International Association for Organ Donation

- **www.seniors.gov**
  Resources from the U.S. government

- **www.MAXIMUMgenerosity.org**
  Research and information from Brian Kluth

## BOOKS

American Bar Association. *The Complete Personal Legal Guide: The Essential Reference for Every Household*. New York, NY: Random House Reference. 2008.

Bennett, Gordon Meade. *How to Avoid Probate by Creating a Living Trust*. New York, NY: Sterling Publishing. 2007.

Cady, Donald F. *Field Guide to Financial Planning*. Erlanger, KY: The National Underwriter Company. 2010.

Cady, Donald F. *Field Guide to Insurance and Employee Benefits*. Erlanger, KY: The National Underwriter Company. 2010.

Cullen, Melanie with Shea Irving. *Get It Together: Organize Your Records So Your Family Won't Have To*. Berkeley, CA: Nolo. 2008.

Graham, Billy. *Nearing Home*. Nashville, TN: Thomas Nelson. 2011

Groopman, Jerome, MD, and Pamela Hartzband, MD. *Your Medical Mind*. New York, NY: The Penguin Press. 2011.

Hanks, Lisa. *The Mom's Guide to Wills and Estate Planning*. Berkeley, CA: Nolo. 2009.

Kiernan, Stephen P. *Last Rites: Rescuing the End of Life from the Medical System*. New York, NY: St. Martin's Press. 2006.

Kubler-Ross, Elizabeth. *On Death and Dying*. New York, NY: Macmillan. 1969.

Larson, Aaron. *Wills and Trusts Kit for Dummies*. Hoboken, NJ: Wylie Publishing Inc. 2008.

Loehr, Jim, and Tony Schwartz. *The Power of Full Engagement*. New York, NY: The Free Press. 2005.

Swindoll, Charles R. *Swindoll's Ultimate Book of Illustrations*. Nashville, TN: Thomas Nelson Publishers. 1998.

# NOTES

1. This book is in memory of Ronald Thomas Craig, September 2, 1944-January 14, 2008.

2. Quote from *The Little Foxes,* page 128, originally published in 1866 but available now from Amazon in an edition from www.bibliobazzar.com/opensource.

3,4. Kluth, Brian, *Because I Love You, Family Organizer,* (Colorado Springs, CO: Maximum Generosity, 2009), 17.

5. Charles R. Swindoll, *Swindoll's Ultimate Book of Quotations* (Nashville, TN: Thomas Nelson, 1998), 392.

6. The Brown Center for Geriatric Studies, "Facts on Dying," http://www.chcr.brown.edu/dying/2001DATA.HTM (accessed April 2010).

7. *The American Bar Association Complete Personal Legal Guide: The Essential Reference for Every Household.* (New York, NY: Random House Reference, 2008), 637.

8. Stephen P. Kiernan, *Last Rites: Rescuing the End of Life from the Medical System.* (New York, NY: St. Martins Press, 2006), 209.

9. American Medical Association, "Cancer Patients Who Get Palliative Care Suffer Less, Study Shows," http://www.palliative-care.net/study (accessed May 2010).

10. American Cancer Society, Medical review 3/8/2011, under "What is hospice care?" http://www.cancer.org/Treatment/FindingandPayingforTreatment/ChoosingYourTreatmentTeam/HospiceCare/hospice-care-what-is-hospice-care (accessed April 14, 2010).

11. "Why are doctors so reluctant to discuss end of life care?" A response by Jimmy Stille, http://www.kevinmd.com/blog/2010/01/doctors-reluctant-discuss-life-care.html (accessed November 9, 2010).

12. "Means to a Better End," http://www.rwjf.org/files/publications/other/meansbetterend.pdf (accessed November 15, 2010).

13. Ron Winslow, "The Revolving Door at the Hospital," *The Wall Street Journal,* June 10, 2010.

14. Lisa Hanks, *The Mom's Guide to Wills and Estate Planning,* (Berkeley, CA: Nolo, 2009), 86

15. Kevin Helliker, "Giving Back an Identity to Donated Cadavers," The Wall Street Journal, February 1, 2011.

16. Laura Daily, "Novel Send-offs to Help Take the Sting Out of Grief," AARP, http://www.aarp.org/relationships/grief-loss/info-06-2008/odd_funeral_requests.html (accessed January, 2010).

17. Jessica Milford, *The American Way of Death* (New York, NY: Vintage Books, a division of Random House, first vintage books edition, 2000). Available in bookstores and on Amazon.com

18. Stephen P. Kiernan, *Last Rights: Rescuing the End of Life from the Medical System.* (New York, NY: St. Martin's Press, 2000), p.275.

19. "Life Insurance Statistics: 35 million Do Not Have Life Insurance," http://www.myinsurancelife.com/life-insurance/life-insurance-statistics-35-million-do-not-have-life-insurance (accessed September, 2010).

20. Mary Beth Franklin, "Insuring Against Life's Frailties" *Kiplinger's Personal Finance Magazine,* July, 1999.

21. Long Term Care Insurance National Advisory Center, http://www.longtermcareinsurance.org (accessed September, 2010).

22. "Your Money," AARP Newsletter, http://www.aarp.org/money/estate-planning/info-2007/funeral_survey.html (accessed January 2011).

23. There are a number of works that discuss Carnegie's position on wealth and philanthropy. One of the most recent is the biography, *Andrew Carnegie* by David Nasaw, copyrighted in 2006 and published by Penguin Press.

24. Michelle Conlin, Lauren Gard, and Jessi Hempel with Kate Hazelwood, David Polek, and Tony Bianco, Special Report Philanthropy, (New York, November 29, 2004), http://www.businessweek.com/magazine/content/04_48/b3910401.htm (accessed February 2009).

25. Randy Alcorn, *The Treasure Principle Bible Study* (Sisters, Oregon: Multnomah Publishers,2003).

26. © 1972 Bud John Songs/EMI Christian Music Publishing. Words by Carol Owen

27. © Richard Kirkland, "Should You Leave It All to the Children?" *Fortune* magazine, November 1986, http://money.cnn.com/magazines/fortune/fortune_archive/1986/09/29/68098/index.htm (accessed January, 2010).

28. CBS Sunday Morning, July 11, 2011.

29. James Patterson, *Spirit* Magazine, Southwest Airlines, June, 2011, 272.

30. Arch Oboler's radio plays, http://otrarchive.blogspot.com/2011/07/arch-obolers-plays.html (accessed August 2011).

31. Stephen R. Covey, *The 7 Habits of Highly Effective People* (New York: Simon and Schuster, 2004). First Things First is the 3rd habit of the 7 habits of highly effective people. This best-selling book is as relevant today as when it was written in 1989.

32. Dr. Henry Cloud, *Necessary Endings* (New York, NY: HarperCollins Publishers Ltd., 2011). Dr. Cloud's book is important reading , not only for business leaders, but for all of us who have difficulty accepting and carrying out "necessary endings" in our lives.

33. "Live Like You Were Dying," words and music by Tim Nichols and Craig Wiseman. Warner Tamburlaine Music, 2004. There is also a book based on the lyrics by the authors of the song, available at Amazon.com or at local bookstores.

34. Jim Loehr and Tony Schwartz, *The Power of Full Engagement* (New York, NY: The Free Press, 2005), 12.

35. A bucket list is a list of things people would like to accomplish before they "kick the bucket." It was popularized in the film *The Bucket List* starring Morgan Freeman and Jack Nicholson.

# INDEX